TWO CLASSES OF MEN

Every man is born an Aristotelian, or a Platonist. I do not think it possible that any one born an Aristotelian can become a Platonist; and I am sure no born Platonist can change into an Aristotelian. They are the two classes of men, besides which it is next to impossible to conceive a third.

S. T. Coleridge,
Specimens of the Table Talk,
2 July 1830

Maurice says it is the great evil of everything at Oxford that there is nothing but Aristotelianism. And I find it was the superiority of Cambridge in this respect that made him think it so much better for me to go to the latter University. Maurice says all little children are Platonists, and it is their education which makes men Aristotelians.

Letter of Edward Strachey to his aunt,
Lady Louis, 27 October 1836.

TWO
CLASSES OF MEN

Platonism and English
Romantic Thought

DAVID NEWSOME

JOHN MURRAY

THE BIRKBECK LECTURES
IN THE UNIVERSITY OF CAMBRIDGE
MAY 1972

Printed in Great Britain by
Butler & Tanner Ltd., Frome and London

0 7195 3087 3

Contents

Preface

It is always interesting to work out how a book took shape in one's mind. The genesis of this particular study goes back to the spring of 1968 when I was working out the links between the Platonism of F. D. Maurice and that of Brooke Foss Westcott, and I first tried to make some sense of the strange conversation between Maurice and Edward Strachey in 1836 which forms the continuing motif of the present book. In May 1968 I gave a lecture at Birmingham University, under the auspices of the Education Department, on Aristotelian Oxford in the nineteenth century. Later in the same year I gave the Westcott Memorial Lecture at Cambridge on the theme of Bishop Westcott's Platonism. In both these lectures I nibbled at some of the implications of Maurice's adaptation of Coleridge's aphorism that 'every man is born an Aristotelian or a Platonist'. In 1969, the Master and Fellows of Trinity College, Cambridge, invited me to deliver the Birkbeck Lectures at Cambridge in the summer of 1972; and this invitation, with the advantage of two sabbatical terms before leaving Cambridge for Christ's Hospital, gave me the opportunity to read more fully into Coleridge and Plato and to work out the deeper implications of Maurice's statement.

My first idea was to write a book and then to adapt it for the Birkbeck Lectures. In the end I felt that the shorter presentation, in the form of the actual lectures, would make for easier reading. I have included some additional material—an introductory essay on Plato and Aristotle and a few appendices of a more technical nature which elaborate or qualify some of the points and generalisations made in the lectures. My thanks are due, firstly, to the Master and Fellows of Trinity for the honour which they paid me; to the Master and Fellows of Emmanuel for granting me two sabbatical terms; to my former colleagues Dr Ronald Gray and the Revd. Don Cupitt for putting up with my intermittent questions about Goethe's

ix

Preface

alchemical pursuits and the idea of *coincidentia oppositorum*; and to Dr John Beer, Fellow of Peterhouse, for much good advice and his helpful suggestions.

I must conclude with two apologies. The first is for taking the terms of the Birkbeck Lectures rather more widely than is customary, in that I have included within the sphere of ecclesiastical history and religious thought such matters as literary criticism, philosophy and cultural history. My defence is simple. In the nineteenth century, thinkers still passionately adhered to the belief in the integration of knowledge, although they would not have called it that. They would have seen at once the futility of considering the development of religious thought without reference to the cultural and philosophical movements of the time. So that is really a false apology. The second, however, is genuine enough; and that is for my pretensions as an historian in venturing into so many other disciplines in order to feed the generalizations which a study of this scope is bound to engender. When Thomas Taylor, the English Platonist, produced his editions of Plato and the Neoplatonists, a reviewer in *Blackwood's Magazine* in 1825 dismissed his labours in unequivocal terms. 'The man is an ass, in the first place', he wrote. 'Secondly he knows nothing of the religion of which he is so great a fool as to profess himself a votary; and thirdly, he knows less than nothing of the language about which he is continually writing.' This happens to be monstrously unjust to Taylor; but the words stand as something of a warning to anyone who would venture into an inter-disciplinary study such as this.

DAVID NEWSOME

Christ's Hospital
March 1973

Introduction

Coleridge was not the first thinker, nor indeed has he been the last, to divide mankind into 'two classes of men'. Heinrich Heine once observed that 'all men are either Jews or Greeks',[1] thus anticipating Matthew Arnold's celebrated dichotomy between Hebraists and Hellenists. Goethe, in the preface to *Farbenlehre*, divided the world into Platonists and Aristotelians, expressing the idea with such ponderous qualification that he forfeited any claim to its originality.[2] W. S. Gilbert, through the philosophical Private Willis, chose as his great divide the innate propensity of man to belong to one of two political parties, the Liberal or the Conservative. Charles Lamb was even more down to earth. There were 'two races of men', he wrote in the *Essays of Elia*—those who borrow and those who lend.[3]

Coleridge was an inveterate borrower—not only of books but of ideas that he culled from them. Often enough he improved upon them too; and markedly so in his own version of Goethe's division between the disciples of the two greatest philosophers of ancient Athens. The remark, as recorded in the *Table Talk* for 2 July 1830, was as follows:

Every man is born an Aristotelian, or a Platonist. I do not think it possible that any one born an Aristotelian can become a Platonist; and I am sure no born Platonist can change into an Aristotelian. They are the two classes of men, besides which it is next to impossible to conceive a third.[4]

The five lectures that follow are all studies on this Coleridgean theme, or—more precisely—on a variant of it by F. D. Maurice during a conversation with his pupil, Edward Strachey, in 1836. It may be helpful, however, at the outset to consider what Coleridge himself meant by this natural division into two ways of thinking in order to elucidate the elaboration of this idea in the studies which form the substance of this book.

Coleridge's chief concern was to distinguish between two

I

ways of defining and establishing truth. How much is it possible for us to know? Is knowledge limited to our reasoning over things which we can see and sense, or is there some higher order of abstract truth, beyond the reach of our senses and the limits of observation, which man can yet apprehend by some higher faculty than the reasoning power? Is knowledge limited to contemplation of finite properties, or can it extend into the realm of the infinite; and—if so—does that knowledge of the infinite give us a deeper insight into the nature of reality itself?

On a brilliant May morning in 1827, Mr Samuel Pickwick threw open his chamber window and contemplated the world around him before setting out on his travels. All that his eye could see in all directions was—Goswell Street.

'Such', thought Mr Pickwick, 'are the narrow views of those philosophers who, content with examining the things that lie before them, look not to the truths which are hidden beyond. As well might I be content to gaze on Goswell Street for ever, without one effort to penetrate to the hidden countries which on every side surround it.'

One does not immediately associate Mr Pickwick with Coleridgeanism, but here in simple language he had expressed the epistemological quest of the Romantics, whether poets, philosophers or theologians; a quest which grew, as all thought must grow, out of the intellectual debates of their times. The leading minds of the late seventeenth and the eighteenth centuries had tended to limit the range of human knowledge to reasoning over observable phenomena. They belonged to the empiricist tradition, ascribed to Aristotle and popularized by the philosopher of sensationalism (i.e. the notion that all ideas come into the mind from outside through sense-impressions), John Locke. During the eighteenth century one can discern a *malaise*, symptomatic of dissatisfaction with this clear-cut, well-defined concept of truth and the means to attain it. At first it lay below the surface, taking the form of a yearning for mystery and a fascination for the occult. This was accompanied by a growing conviction that ideas were really innate and reflective of some higher infinite order of reality which lay beyond the reach of sense-impressions. Truth must be more than merely meets the eye. Eternal mysteries can be intuitively grasped.

Introduction

The certainty of this fact led thinkers to the philosophical system which Locke himself had attacked—to the seventeenth-century Platonists, who wrote of 'the mind's eye' as opposed to the naked eye, and of apprehension of the world of *noumena*, the abstract, infinite order of things, as opposed to understanding of the material phenomena of the actual world in which men live. Thus they came to Plato himself for deliverance from the limited epistemology of Aristotle and Locke.

This was the intellectual context of Romanticism, which was itself the upsurge of this previously-subdued spirit, confident in the claims of the visionary power, the intuitive faculty in man, to unfold the deepest secrets of the universe. It is hardly surprising that the Romantics should conceive of themselves as standing in a class apart. There were Aristotelians whose sight was restricted by blinkers. There were Platonists who perceived a higher way to truth. Even Kant, according to Coleridge, suffered from restricted vision, since—although he acknowledged the existence of *noumena* beyond the material world of phenomena—he had stated that the rational contemplation of the *noumena* was limited to Practical Reason, which could only determine 'regulative' truth (rules of action) but not 'constitutive' truth—the knowledge of things in themselves.

So Coleridge himself explained further his division of all thinkers into Aristotelians and Platonists:

The one considers reason a quality, or attribute; the other considers it a power. I believe that Aristotle never could get to understand what Plato meant by an idea. . . . With Plato ideas are constitutive in themselves. Aristotle was, and still is, the sovereign lord of the Understanding; the faculty judging by the senses. He was a conceptualist, and never could raise himself into that higher state, which was natural to Plato, and has been so to others, in which the understanding is distinctly contemplated, and, as it were looked down upon from the throne of ideas, as living, inborn, essential truths. Yet what a mind was Aristotle's—only not the greatest that ever animated the human form!—the parent of science, properly so called the master of criticism, and the founder or editor of logic! But he confused science with philosophy, which is an error. Philosophy is the middle state between science, or knowledge, and sophia, or wisdom.[5]

3

Doubtless time, and the emergence of two distinct traditions, have exaggerated the differences between Plato and Aristotle in their understanding of the nature of truth. After all, Aristotle was Plato's pupil. He absorbed a great deal more from Plato than he rejected, and their common teaching has been so thoroughly absorbed into Western Christian thought that it is often difficult to distinguish the allegedly rival points of view. Throughout history, however, there has been a tendency to regard Plato as the prophet of poetic truth as compared to Aristotle who was the great original of the scientific mind. Basil Willey, for instance, has reminded us that in Raphael's painting, Plato looks up to heaven, while 'Aristotle bends his head downwards'.[6] An Aristotelian might say that the one has his head in the clouds, while the other is firmly rooted in the world of practical experience. This, however, is a superficial distinction, in some way explained by the fortuitous circumstance that Plato's works have survived in their original presentation —the poetic-dialogue form with characters of flesh and blood— while Aristotle's have not. What to Cicero was a 'golden stream' of rhetorical writing has been irretrievably lost,[7] and Aristotle's work has survived only in the form of treatises and lecture notes.

Nevertheless Aristotle cannot really be disguised as a Platonist. His concept of the nature of truth and the means of apprehending it differed from Plato's in five significant respects. The first is fundamental. Aristotle could not accept the validity of innate ideas. If philosophers can be divided into two schools— those whose starting-point is the reality of the subject, the thinking mind itself, and those who regard the mind as a *tabula rasa* which cannot think until bombarded by sense-impressions from material objects outside it—then Plato and Aristotle stand at the two poles. How Plato convinced himself that the mind could have knowledge of things in themselves prior to, or irrespective of, experience of the material world will be discussed in the course of these studies. But because he believed that this was the case, his whole approach to the problem of identifying reality differed fundamentally from that of Aristotle.

This brings us to the second point of difference. Plato believed in the existence of an ideal world of Forms or Universals, beyond the visible world in which we actually live. These Forms were the original ideas of all created things—divine and immutable within the eternal order, but finite and changing within the temporal, visible world. The actual world may be ugly, confused, nonsensical—a pointer to the degree to which finite minds can forget or depart from the divine original; so that as time passes, they believe that the formless mockery of their own invention is in fact reality, when it is only a shadow or reflection of the perfection which once had been and actually (within the eternal order) still is. If knowledge of reality were purely an empirical process, the real world of Forms could never be apprehended by man. Here Platonists tended to elaborate upon their master, in the elevation of the role of intuition to penetrate the veil which separated the finite from the infinite, phenomena from *noumena*. They might call the process different names—intuition, 'the mind's eye', vision or imagination—but they were all confident that once the veil was pierced, confusion would become order, ugliness would become beauty, the indefinite would acquire measure and the many would be seen as one.

This was not Aristotle's language. While he drew a distinction between *sophia* and *phronesis*, the speculative power and moral tact or experience, he came more and more concerned in his later writings with the quest for the attainable rather than speculating on the nature of the one universal good. Here, more than anywhere else, Aristotle revealed his preoccupation with the practical rather than the speculative. *Phronesis* came to play the all-important part in his thought. A moral sense is acquired through the experience of living rightly, and right action is itself a sort of practical wisdom, a lived truth. Hence 'the good man judges in every instance correctly'; quality of life determines quality of thought, a more cautious and more practical induction than the stark Platonic conclusion that virtue and knowledge are in reality the same thing.[8]

The third distinction concerns the concept of nature and the process of time. To Plato the true nature of every created thing is revealed in its origin and is therefore best understood by a study of its beginning. Following from this, the movement of time must necessarily imply declension, for if an object is created perfect, subsequent change or development (the condition of the finite world) can only lead to imperfection. Aristotle's standpoint was the precise opposite. To him, the law of nature was dynamic. Everything created by nature has a purpose to fulfil; and this is realized in its consummated state, its *telos*, its end. Therefore to understand the nature of any object or quality which is being studied, one must find out what the object is becoming rather than what it has been. Both the essence and the purpose are revealed in the final state rather than in the original creation. Hence Aristotle regarded change and development as a law of life. Plato regarded it as the condition of the finite world, which must become less and less consonant with the eternal, immutable world of Forms.

The last two distinctions which ought to be mentioned relate to the location of truth and the means whereby it might be verified. To Aristotle, truth is seen as a middle position or mean between two extremes. It partakes of the quality of virtue which is itself a mean between an excess of a quality and its corresponding deficiency (so courage, the second cardinal virtue, is the mean between foolhardiness and cowardice)[9]. Plato's teaching cannot be defined so exactly. His followers, however, notably the Renaissance Platonists, interpreted the teaching of Plato's later Dialogues as substantiating that truth is really a *coincidentia oppositorum*, rather than a mean, a state of reconciliation of opposites, embracing both poles at once, so that truth can never be in a middle position and must always lie at both extremes. This problem, as will be seen later, fascinated the Romantics (and Coleridge in particular) who threw Plato's caution to the winds and proclaimed *coincidentia oppositorum* as a universal law.

The fifth point of difference follows from this. If truth is really some divine reconciliation of opposites, a harmony of the apparent diversities which puzzle the mass of men, then the revelation of its secret workings may be vouchsafed only to a select few. The mass of men could not acquire this *gnosis*. They would not understand it. As Plato himself said, the multitude cannot be philosophical.[10] To the philosopher, as to the artist, truth is self-authenticating. The Platonic philosopher

6

knows when he has a vision of truth, although he may never be able to convince the mass of men that he has been able to transcend the limited vision of the many. Aristotle did not employ esoteric (or, in political terms, élitist) language. To Aristotle, truth can be verified by common experience, by general assent. What the mass of men accept as right *is* usually right. Therefore collective wisdom, especially on matters of ethics, has a power and a validity which Plato could never have acknowledged.[11] Perhaps in this sense, Aristotle has some claim to be accounted the first Whig.

All these distinctions, together with others, will be elaborated in the studies that follow. They should not be taken as exhaustive. There is, however, one further difficulty in generalizing about Platonists and Aristotelians in the context of more modern times. Both philosophers were founders of a system; and the original Platonic and Aristotelian deposits were added to and embellished by a succession of disciples and pseudo-disciples over the ages. The schoolmen systematized Aristotle; the Neo-Platonists presumed to clarify the obscurities of Plato, to fill in the gaps and to adapt his teaching to gnostic and Christian doctrines. Much, then, of what one meets in Romantic Platonism is nearer to Plotinus than to Plato. With almost every allegedly Platonic idea which is examined in the chapters to come—the Romantic conception of intuition, the application of *anamnesis* to children, the law of polarity or *coincidentia oppositorum*—such elaboration will be seen to have taken place. Even Coleridge, who was so insistent on the need not to confound Plotinism with Platonism,[12] would call Plato to witness to a Neoplatonic doctrine. The more one studies English Romantic thought, with all its self-conscious Hellenism and its bewildering variety of extemporization of ancient Athenian themes, the more inclined one is to agree with John Morley's shrewd observation: 'Assuredly not every one who saith "Plato, Plato" is admitted to that intellectual kingdom.'[13]

1

Plato and the Romantics

In a letter to his aunt, dated 27 October 1836, Edward Strachey recalled a conversation which he had recently had with Frederick Denison Maurice. They had been discussing together whether Strachey should prepare himself for entry to the University of Oxford. Maurice had had some doubt. 'It is the great evil of everything at Oxford,' he had said to Strachey, 'that there is nothing but Aristotelianism.' At Cambridge, on the other hand, he would be better served by encountering the rival tradition of Platonism. Strachey, who was an apt pupil and knew his Coleridge well, had thrown back at Maurice the Coleridgean adage that all men are either Platonists or Aristotelians from their birth. But Maurice would not have this at all. 'All little children are Platonists,' he had replied, 'and it is their education which makes men Aristotelians.'[1]

The five studies that follow are an attempt to elucidate this remark, and to try to answer certain other important questions for an historian of ideas which are forced upon him in the course of such an enquiry. What did Coleridge mean by his aphorism? Is it true that the rival universities belonged to or cherished two different philosophical systems? What was the Platonism which Maurice himself imbibed through Julius Hare at Cambridge, and Hare from Coleridge? Was it really a sort of bastard Platonism, as transmitted by the Neoplatonists? What did Maurice mean by his ascription to children of a natural Platonism? What did an Aristotelian education imposed upon a naturally Platonic mind give to a consummate Oxford genius such as John Henry Newman? Finally, in what respects did this Platonism colour or shape the theology of the nineteenth century?

There are two prior considerations, however. The first is an indisputable fact. The second is a question arising from it. The fact is this: F. D. Maurice's observation is a peculiarly nineteenth-century remark. It would have been both untrue and meaningless had it been made a century earlier; firstly, because neither Oxford nor Cambridge was steeped in Greek learning; secondly, because his observation about the natural vision or wisdom of a child was a peculiar conceit of the cultural movement known as Romanticism. So the question which has to be answered is, what is the connection between the philosophy of Plato and the emergence of Romanticism?

Readers of Dr R. M. Ogilvie's stimulating study *Latin and Greek* will not be likely to dispute his general thesis—that the eighteenth century in England witnessed a predominantly Latin culture, with Horace as the *beau ideal*, giving way to a self-consciously Greek culture at the time of the Romantic movement.[2] This does not mean that the ideas of the Greeks were forgotten in the eighteenth century. As Professor Noto-poulos has observed, in his study of Shelley, it is perfectly possible to be a Platonist without knowing it,[3] just as it is possible to think oneself a Platonist without actually being one. It was doubtless with this first consideration in mind that Shelley wrote his famous words in the preface to *Hellas*: 'We are all Greeks. Our Laws, our literature, our religion, our arts, have their root in Greece.'[4] As far as the eighteenth century was concerned, the legacy of Greece had been absorbed uncon-sciously; or, as Wordsworth said to Emerson in 1848, in reply to the question—would Plato's *Republic* find many readers if published as a new book?—'No; and yet,' after a thoughtful pause, 'we have embodied it all.'[5]

But Platonism is a perennial philosophy and it cannot die. In the eighteenth century, therefore, both in England and on the Continent, it is to be sought beneath the surface, amidst the esoteric tradition. As a useful rule of thumb, it may be said, where there is pietism, there will be Platonism or—at least—a form of Platonism. In Germany, the chief source of the Neo-platonic tradition in the eighteenth century was Jacob Boehme, especially his *Aurora*, which was studied by Goethe, Novalis, Hegel and Schopenhauer; and beyond Boehme lay Paracelsus and the occult wisdom of the Cabbala and the Hermetic

Tradition. Jacob Boehme, in fact, was the one indisputably common influence upon the Romantic Platonists of Germany and England alike; and his teaching was a curious amalgam of Anabaptist teaching on the 'inner light', alchemical symbolism and imagery, and the doctrine of Paracelsus on the 'signatures' (the notion, derived with mystical elaboration from the *Parmenides* and the *Timaeus*, that since reality existed only in the invisible world, the actual visible world in which we live must bear within it marks, signs, correspondences or 'signatures' of the ideal world of which it is the shadow).

Many studies have been made, in recent years, of this union of pietism with the occult—by Frances Yates, Desirée Hirst and M. H. Abrams—but I have yet to find a shrewder and more judicious analysis of the interconnection between occultism and pietism than in Dr Ronald Gray's study of the alchemical influences upon Goethe. He writes as follows:

Alchemy, as Goethe came to know it, was professed mainly by Christian teachers; it was one branch of that mystical Pietism represented by Boehme, Gottfried Arnold and Susanna von Klettenburg. There was nothing contradictory in this association with Christianity. The fundamental ethical ideas of the alchemists, that the way to a higher life lay through the straight gate, is fundamental also to the Christian religion. But it is not an exclusively Christian belief. Where the Christian differs from other believers is in his insistence that the way was shown by divine example; by the self-sacrifice of God at a historical point in time. This is not a part of alchemical doctrine, although it is possible to introduce it there, as the Pietists observed.[6]

German Romantic Platonism was nurtured on Behmenism and pietism. The next stage was to explore the roots. So Novalis went back to Plotinus, and Schleiermacher (whose mind was formed within the tradition of Moravian pietism) back to Plato himself in his monumental translation with Friedrich Schlegel of the Dialogues.

We see exactly the same pattern in England during the eighteenth century. The influence of Jacob Boehme came through William Law, to be absorbed for its pietism and spirituality, so reminiscent of the Cambridge Platonists of the

seventeenth century, by the Wesleys; and for its Neoplatonism
and occultism by the Swedenborgians and the circle into which
Flaxman and William Blake were drawn towards the end of
the century. And as the canonical texts themselves were appear-
ing in Germany together with contemporary commentaries
(Mendelssohn's study of the *Phaedo* in 1767 was a landmark
here), so too in England with the researches of Thomas Taylor,
Floyer Sydenham and Ebenezer McFaite.

This endeavour to rediscover Plato coincided with a re-
newed interest in the antiquities of Greece which began with
the disclosures in the 1730's and 1740's of the buried towns of
Herculaneum and Pompeii, followed by the publication of
Stuart and Revett's *Antiquities of Athens* and the translation by
Henry Fuseli of Abbé Winkelmann's *Reflections on the Paintings
and Sculptures of the Greeks*. The intellectual excitement aroused
by these discoveries and researches was, Joseph Barrell has
written, 'comparable to the discovery of Greek literature in the
fifteenth century. . . . For a thousand years the ancients had
been thought of as characters in a tale. Now it was possible to
look at their daily lives, to see their art in quantity and in
colour. . . . The ancient world had come alive.'[7] Certainly
there was a sort of humanistic exuberance in the young
Shelley when he first encountered the *Symposium* or in his
admiration for T. L. Peacock, close enough friend of Thomas
Taylor to have received from him the absurd, though significant, nickname of 'Greeky-Peaky'. 'How is Peaky with his
Greeky?' he once presumed to ask.[8]

It is curious how little contemporary German influence—
except through the translation of Winkelmann—is seen in this
growing English interest in Greek culture and Platonic philosophy. In fact it was not until the 1790's that any attention
whatever was paid to intellectual movements in Germany, and
then only to the mystery dramas, the *Schicksalstragödie* of
Schiller, mainly through the efforts of Henry Mackenzie who
chose to lecture on this subject before the Royal Society of
Edinburgh in 1788.[9] The chief propagandist on behalf of
German studies, and most particularly the writings of the
transcendentalists, was Henry Crabb Robinson, the friend of
William Blake and all the Lake poets—part dilettante, part

intermediary—who delighted to find in both Wordsworth's and Coleridge's minds a marked German bent.[10]

At the very end of the century, when Coleridge had mastered the German language, he began to learn from Kant and Schelling, but precisely *what* he learnt is very difficult to say. He owed nothing to the Germans for his Neoplatonism, because this he had encountered in his reading of Plotinus and Iamblichus as a Grecian at Christ's Hospital. My own belief is this: the influence of Kant and Schelling on Coleridge was twofold. In the first place, Coleridge was brought back by them to his earliest intellectual enthusiasm, after a temporary flirtation with Necessitarianism. He was returning to the Platonic stock, as it were, in his growing enthusiasm for Berkeley and Boehme, and at that stage he encountered Kant, whose writings took possession of his mind 'as with a giant's hand'.[11] This is surely what Coleridge meant when he wrote of Kant's influence upon him, that it was 'more formal than material—to have resided rather in the scientific statement of convictions *previously attained* than in the acquisition of new truths'.[12]

Secondly, Coleridge learnt from Kant and Schelling a philosophical terminology—the distinction between Reason and Understanding, the peculiar sense which he attached to the word Imagination—and then applied this terminology to a structure of thought, basically Platonist in its principles, which owed little or nothing to the Germans. At the beginning of the nineteenth century there was emerging a common philosophical vocabulary, as attempts were made to articulate or to define such concepts as the relationship between thought and reason, the limits of human understanding, the source of moral convictions and the inter-communion (or lack of it) between the finite and the infinite. Nowhere is this better shown than in E. D. Hirsch's comparative study of Wordsworth and Schelling. Both were enunciating a nature-philosophy in terms of reconciliation rather than alienation; both were seeking to define some sort of dynamic principle which was at work within the universe; yet neither was familiar with the writings of the other. Hirsch came to what he believed to be the only possible conclusion, that 'to explain the similarities of the two writers we are thrown back on the simple hypothesis that Wordsworth and Schelling developed independently an identical *Weltan-schauung*.[13]

To use such a term as *Weltanschauung* practically amounts—as far as the historian is concerned—to an admission of defeat. But it is better to admit defeat than to suggest a positive influence which cannot in fact have existed. It is well to remember, too, that evidence that one thinker has read the works of another is not proof that his thought is subsequently moulded by what he has read. He may read the work in the light of some conclusion already formed in his own mind. In just such a way did Coleridge misunderstand the use by Schelling of the word *Einbildungskraft* as meaning 'multeity in unity', or the 'esemplastic' function of the imagination.[14] And when he came to Kant, Coleridge's immediate disposition was to categorize him. He must put him into one of 'the two classes of men', either a Platonist or an Aristotelian. Because he believed that ideas were 'regulative only', Kant was labelled by Coleridge a 'Conceptionist' as opposed to an 'Ideist', a child of Aristotle rather than a true spiritual child of Plato.[15] 'No born Platonist', Coleridge wrote, 'can ever change into an Aristotelian.'[16] So, as far as Coleridge was concerned, Kant might be respected as a teacher, but he could never be a master.

But we must return to the main argument. Platonism was escaping from its esoteric obscurity towards the end of the eighteenth century. It was to become the lifeblood of Romanticism; or, as Professor G. M. Harper has put it, 'the revival of interest in Plato . . . may be the most important single facet of the Romantic movement.'[17] Why was this so? The main reason would appear to be the operation of a natural intellectual dialectic—the swinging of the pendulum in the realm of ideas. If we call it 'the flight from Reason', we mean by that the attempt to extricate oneself and one's contemporaries from the barren and cold concept of reason as taught by John Locke and accepted by the age of Enlightenment. Expressed more philosophically, it is an attempt to transcend the bounds of understanding by exploring the realms of the infinite. The Romantics believed that their generation had been guided by men whose sight was restricted by blinkers, who confined the search for truth to an empirical process, having been taught

Two Classes of Men

that the mind was a *tabula rasa*, that there was no such thing
as an innate idea, that the safest and surest guide for a con-
structive and objective philosophy was the tag of Newton—
hypotheses non fingo. One of the first to reject this limited
vision was William Blake; and, after him, Coleridge who
pointed to the source of a deeper knowledge of the universe
which his contemporaries had neglected. 'Plato . . . the divine
Plato', he wrote, 'was not to be comprehended within the field
of vision, or be commanded by the fixed immoveable telescope
of Mr Locke's human understanding.'[18] And again, in his *Philosophical Lectures* delivered in the winter of 1818: 'I am happy
to see and feel that men are craving for a better diet than the
wretched trash they have been fed with for the last century.'[19]

A reaction against the sensationalism of Locke, or—as Coleridge saw it—the empiricism of Aristotle which lay behind it,
would naturally lead thinkers to a closer study of the rival
philosophical tradition, to Plato and his disciples. But it goes
deeper than that. If Lockean understanding were a formal
garden, landscaped with delicacy, all ordered and trim, then
those who despised such a sight as a conceit and an artifice
would turn their eyes to the undergrowth and the wilderness.
Rejecting flowers, they will look for weeds. If they know in
their hearts that truth is more than meets the eye, they will shun
the open and the obvious, and will go questing for mystery,
the grotesque and the arcane.

The genesis of Romanticism is exactly this. It is both a looking back into earlier truths—mythology, legends, secret cults—
and a looking beyond to the sagas of the North and the occultism of the East. Romanticism begins with a taste for curiosities
and a passion for thrills. The young Coleridge was allegedly
reading Boehme's *Aurora* and Mallet's *Northern Antiquities* while
at Christ's Hospital.[20] Those who have studied John Livingston Lowes' classic on the sources of the *Ancient Mariner* and
Kubla Khan will hardly need reminding of Coleridge's ensuing
quests into the exotic and the occult; and when the German
mystery dramas hit London, Coleridge was the first to sing
their praises. Reviewing Matthew Gregory Lewis' grotesque
extravaganza *The Monk*, he summed it up with the dramatic
punch-line: 'the tale of the bleeding nun is truly terrific'.[21]

This mood, and these researches, led the early Romantics to the Platonic tradition in all its forms—the seventeenth-century divines, the alchemists, Paracelsus and Bruno, the classical Neoplatonists, and of course Plato himself. And within that tradition they found their answer to Locke.

*   *   *

The key to the new epistemology lies in the Romantics' use of the word 'imagination'. As Mr Flosky in *Nightmare Abbey* (a very thinly disguised Coleridge) vouchsafed to poor Marionetta, 'this distinction between fancy and imagination is one of the most abstruse and important points in metaphysics. I have written several hundred pages of promise to elucidate it.'[22]

Somewhat less ambitiously we may say that the Romantic poets conceived of imagination as being the property of all men. Wordsworth described himself as 'a man speaking to men'.[23] Coleridge saw the *primary* imagination as 'the living Power and prime agent of all human perception'.[24] It is true that some people—poets, artists, philosophers—may have a higher perception, but this is really only a difference of degree rather of kind. This higher perception, the possession of which gave the artist a peculiar insight into reality, was described by Coleridge as the secondary imagination. This would appear to have three main attributes.

The first attribute refers to its *modus operandi*. As Coleridge puts it, the secondary imagination 'dissolves, diffuses, dissipates in order to recreate';[25] or—to use the language of the medieval papacy—there is a 'binding and loosing power', perhaps more properly, a 'loosing and binding' power. What this means is that an artist must impose a new unity on what he sees, but this he can only do by disintegrating the superficial unity which may first appear to the eye and then rebinding the parts into a new whole. This is not the mechanistic approach of

> viewing all objects unremittingly
> In disconnection dead and spiritless;
> And still dividing and dividing still.[26]

It is rather what Blake means when he says that a knowledge of particularity must always precede apprehension of the whole; or Shelley, when he writes that 'Reason is the enumeration of quantities already known; imagination is the perception of the value of these quantities, *but separately and as a whole*.'[27] Individuation must precede integration; it is part of the 'esemplastic' process (to use Coleridge's idiosyncratic word) towards the 'completed form of all completeness', as Keats described it in *Endymion*.

The second attribute of imagination is its faculty of unfolding the vision of the One. That the Romantics were preoccupied with unity or oneness is not in itself surprising, and their various expressions of yearning for the One underlying the Many, and the principle of unity which is concealed amidst a world of chaos and confusion, arose fundamentally from their concern for measure; not in the eighteenth-century sense of man's ordered control over the forces of nature, but rather in the sense of the Platonic teaching on the nature of Forms and Universals.

This is very marked in Blake, for instance, who made a fundamental distinction between opinions and principles. Any one could change his opinions; principles remain ever the same.[28] Opinions belong to the world of shadows, principles to the real world of Forms. He could quote Plotinus as testimony: 'That which is altogether destitute of measure is primarily evil'; or Proclus—'The one is measured and bounded, but the multitude . . . is indefinite.'[29] Measure—'the bounding outline'— preserves individuation, the essence of the oak from that of the beech, the horse from the ox.[30] Expressed as a generalization, 'Truth has bounds, Error none.'[31] Perfection, truth, is a unity; it is a circle as the sun is a circle. With a reference to Orphic symbolism, Blake pictures the world as an egg, the perfect gone awry, as in the 'Egg-form'd World of Los'.[32]

This was not peculiar to Blake. Professor William Walsh points out that in the language of the mature Wordsworth, 'suggestions of depth and mystery' are always accompanied by the note of 'sobriety and discipline'.[33]

> The mind of man is fram'd even like the breath
> And harmony of music. There is a dark
> Invisible workmanship that reconciles
> Discordant elements, and makes them move
> In one society.[34]

Many years later, John Ruskin wrote the following memorable words: 'The really precious things are thought and sight, not pace. . . . It does . . . a man, if he be truly a man, no harm to go slow; for his glory is not at all in going, but in being.'[35] All students of nineteenth-century thought will have encountered this note before. It is the common warning, articulated so often within the Railway Age, against equating speed with progress and change with reform. Expressed as it was by John Ruskin, or in similar terms by his contemporary Matthew Arnold, it was sound Platonism.

To the Platonist, the world of Forms was the world of being; the finite world was the world of going. If in the age of Cronos, as pictured by Plato in *The Statesman*, the world of Forms was the actual world,[36] then development thereform into the age of Zeus must have involved declension. Movement from the perfect can only be towards the imperfect. It is in the nature of the One to be changeless. 'When the creator had given all these commands he remained in his own nature.'[37] In the 'feast of contradictions', to use Jowett's phrase, which go up to form the *Parmenides*, the one clear notion that can be derived is that the One, whether it be existent or non-existent, is indivisible and rests in the same place.[38] Being, therefore, as opposed to going, requires—as Keats put it—'fellowship with essence'. Pure thought, that to which the imagination leads, is contemplation of the One, which is itself the Whole. In a sense it is the only thing *worth* contemplating, for—in Shelley's words—'the One remains, the many change and pass'.[39]

This preoccupation with the One as supplying both measure and the universal, unchanging truth, which lay behind the fleeting phenomena of the finite world, naturally led to the attempt to articulate that truth by some all-embracing formula which might stand as the law of the universe. And however the law was defined, it had, somehow, to relate Oneness and changelessness, the essential attributes of the infinite, to multeity and dynamism which seemed to be the condition of all living organisms. Of all the paradoxes with which the Romantics troubled themselves, this was the central one. 'I would make a pilgrimage to the Deserts of Arabia', Coleridge wrote in one of his notebooks, 'to find the man who could make us understand how the *one can be many*! Eternal, universal mystery!'[40]

If the one can be many, and the many one, there must be some interpenetration of the finite world of multeity by the infinite itself. This belief in the power to perceive the infinite within the finite is the third attribute of the Romantic imagination which we are attempting to define.

How could such a power operate? Was it just a question of *Feeling*, as it is expressed in *Endymion*?

> Feel we these things? that moment we have stept
> Into a sort of oneness, and our state
> Is like a fleeting spirit's.[41]

Or is it some sixth sense—a 'sense and taste for the Infinite', as Schleiermacher expressed it, using the word *Gefühl*? It is something about which the Germans had a great deal to say. Schelling, for instance, pointed to the role of *Gemüt*, spirit, mind or heart, which was really little different from what Schleiermacher was saying. 'When we look at things', Schelling wrote, 'and do not perceive the essence within them, but only the empty, abstract forms, then they say nothing to our inner being. We must apply our own spirit, our own *Gemüt* to them, that they shall answer us.'[42] Hegel, seeing the danger of emotional subjectivism, explained in the *Logic* that the process is much more intellectual:

The merely felt and sensible ... is not the spiritual; its heart of hearts is in thought; and only spirit can know spirit. . . . The form of feeling is the lowest in which spiritual truth can be expressed. The world of spiritual existences, God himself, exists in proper truth, only in thought and as thought. If this be so, therefore, thought . . . is the highest and . . . the sole mode of apprehending the eternal and absolute.[43]

It is not heart alone, nor head alone (most of the Romantics would say). It is rather union of heart and head. Truth must be felt upon the pulses. *Le coeur a ses raisons, que la raison ne connait pas.* 'My opinion is this', Coleridge wrote to his friend Thomas Poole in March 1801, 'that deep Thinking is attainable only by a man of deep Feeling, and that all Truth is a species of Revelation.'[44]

Now how Platonic is this line of thinking? Plato gives two answers to the question, how can the finite mind have any knowledge of the infinite? Firstly, it already possesses it in the shape of innate ideas; secondly, there is a process of gaining it through the highest intellectual exercise of dialectic. Dialectic was the only method of gaining true knowledge, or (more exactly) of recovering true knowledge by the correct process of extracting it through the right logical questions from some recollection of the vision of the eternal order which had been vouchsafed to the soul in its pre-existent state.

Protarchus asked Socrates directly in the *Philebus*: 'What is dialectic?' Socrates replied:

Clearly the science which could know all that knowledge of which we are now speaking (the relationship between one and the many); for I am sure that all men who have a grain of intelligence will admit that the knowledge which has to do with being and reality, and sameness and unchangeableness, is by far the truest of all.[45]

All the Platonic dialogues demonstrate the method of dialectic. In the *Republic* it is represented as the final and most searching educational training of the Guardians, and it was the means by which the philosopher discovered that the world of appearances was purely a world of shadows. The highest form of cognition for the mass of men who were enslaved to phenomena was belief or opinion. Knowledge could only be of reality—the Forms existing beyond the world of appearances.[46]

Nowhere is this dialectical process represented as either simple or immediate. Diotima tells Socrates in the *Symposium* that to discover the meaning of true love is a wearisome quest, and can only be attained by a chain of enquiries and experiences 'in due order and succession'. When the discovery comes, the perception is sudden, but it would never come like a flash of inspiration without previous toil.[47] Truth is light, revelation; even the blinding light of the sun, as pictured in the allegory of the Cave; but it cannot come to the soul who has not striven to find it after long rigour. Coleridge, of all the Romantics, understood this best. 'Ignorance seldom vaults into knowledge', he wrote, in *The Friend*, 'but passes into it through an intermediate state of obscurity, even as night into day through twilight.'[48]

Nevertheless all the Romantics were faced with something of a dilemma here. While they employed the image or the myth of pre-existence and *anamnesis*, they could not honestly present this as the foundation of their belief in the intuitive power. There was the fact of their imagination and all that it could reveal. The Platonic tradition was, however, a more fruitful source for intuitional theories outside the intellectual rigours of dialectic. Plotinus, in the *Fifth Ennead* had employed mystical language in his definition of the faculty of discerning spiritual truth:

> It is not lawful to enquire from whence it sprang, as if it were a thing subject to place and motion, for it neither approached hither, nor again departs from hence to some other place; but it either appears to us or it does not appear. So we ought not to pursue it with a view to detecting its secret source, but to watch in quiet till it suddenly shines upon us; preparing ourselves for the blessed spectacle as the eye waits patiently for the rising sun.[49]

This is Blake's language rather than Coleridge's; for the temper that Plotinus evokes is exactly that state of watching and waiting which prompted Blake's reply to the young artist who came to him for advice on 'finding his invention flag'. Gilchrist described the scene. 'Blake turned to his wife and said, "It is just so with us, is it not, for weeks together, when the visions forsake us? What do we do then, Kate?" "We kneel down and pray, Mr Blake" ' was the reply.[50]

Coleridge, although he had studied Plotinus, did not regard himself as a disciple, at least in his maturer years; and he was wont to make a distinction between Platonists and Plotinists with a clear indication of his preference for the former. Even so, while not accepting all the implications of Plotinus' theory of Emanations, he appears to have adopted the Plotinian conception of the Absolute as an 'infinite power pouring itself forth like the sun as from an inexhaustible fullness'.[51]

It would seem that none of the Romantics could be pure Platonists, and for very good reasons. In the first place, too much elaboration of Platonic philosophy had taken place over the centuries for them to be able very clearly to distinguish between what was original and what was justifiable interpretation. It is not only that the Taylor translations and commentaries were impregnated with Neoplatonic imagery and sentiment; in addition to this, they had most of them studied the idealism of Berkeley and had been helped out of the Lockean position by a subjective concept of perception which could easily fit into the framework of Platonic teaching. 'To be is to be perceived' made the human mind the determinant of reality; and when a refined and artistic mind perceived objects in a completely different light and relationship from what the mass of men could discern, it was natural enough to explain the phenomenon in the terms of Plato's allegory of the Cave. So we find Blake combining Berkeley and Plato in the famous statement: 'Mental Things are alone Real; what is called Corporeal, Nobody knows of its Dwelling Place; it is in Fallacy, and its Existence an Imposture. Where is the Existence Out of Mind or Thought? Where is it but in the Mind of a Fool?'[52] Or again, 'Vision or Imagination is a Representation of what Eternally Exists, Really and Unchangeably.' It constitutes 'in that Eternal World the Permanent Realities of Every Thing which we see reflected in this Vegetable Glass of Nature'.[53]

Shelley constantly employed the image of the Veil, that which conceals the ideal world of reality from the mutable world of illusion, sometimes with clear reference to Spenser, and certainly on one occasion with a distinct reference to Berkeley, when he writes of 'penetrating the veil of language to the world of ideas'.[54] Could there be anything more Platonic than the sonnet of 1818, beginning 'Lift not the painted veil which those who live call life . . .'; or than the cave symbolism of *Prometheus Unbound*, where the Cave of Prometheus is contrasted with that of Demogorgan, and Asia cries 'the veil has fallen' as the light streams into the cave of shadows, only to dazzle her even as Plato's prisoners were dazzled.[55]

Neoplatonism and the Berkleian theory of perception offered to the Romantics the immediacy of vision they craved for. It was through this vision that finite objects could reveal or reflect infinite truths. All things, as Coleridge was to put it

21

(echoing a phrase of Cudworth), 'counterfeit infinity'.[56] The quest begins with the eye, but finishes in the mind. It may be that what one looks for is the smallest of things, what may at first appear to be only an accident, not the essence. Yet if all things counterfeit infinity, everything may be taken as symbolical. We come again to the image of 'loosing and binding'. To find the infinite within the finite is to comprehend the particularity of things, which themselves reflect the perfect Whole, the one behind the many. As it was memorably expressed by Blake in *The Last Judgment*:

> He who wishes to see a Vision, a perfect Whole,
> Must see it in its Minute Particulars, Organised.[57]

Then again, from the marginalia to Reynolds' *Discourses*: 'Strictly speaking, all Knowledge is Particulars, To Generalize is to be an Idiot.'[58]

The imagination or vision must see the true nature of the particulars before it can see the harmony and integration within the infinite order. Milton Percival therefore defines Blake's concept of imagination in terms very similar to that of Coleridge's description in the *Biographia Literaria*. It is the quality 'which makes particulars both universal and distinct';[59] that is to say, in functional terms, the quality which enables one to loose before one can bind.

This concern for the particular does not mean, in this context, the scientific or empirical process of establishing categories, but rather the belief that the particular, either through its symbolical nature or because it suddenly impinges upon the mind with a vividness and clarity never before discerned, can illuminate some infinite or eternal truth. In Wordsworthian language, there are sublime moments, 'spots of time', when a single natural object—'one bright star above Seat Sandal and Helvellyn'[60]—can evoke some profound and unlooked-for truth.

> One impulse from a vernal wood
> May teach you more of man,
> Of moral evil and of good,
> Than all the sages can.[61]

Professor Northrop Frye, writing of Blake's 'vision' and its
relation to the limited sight of the empiricists, contrasts the
'world of sight', in which 'we see what we have to see',
with the world of vision, in which 'we see what we want to
see'.[62]

'We see what we want to see.' And what may that be?

> To see a World in a grain of sand,
> And a Heaven in a wild flower,
> Hold Infinity in the palm of your hand,
> And Eternity in an hour.[63]

The distinction between the smallest object in God's creation
and the vastness of the creation itself was not an uncommon
figure. Coleridge uses it, for instance, in *Aids to Reflection*.[64] To
Blake, however, the 'grain of sand' has a cosmic significance.
It is not only that it is itself a part of the divine dispersion or
emanation, which all nature was and therefore still is; it also
reflects the Creator, who, according to the Neoplatonic tradition, endowed all creation with something of a celestial nature.

> Each grain of sand,
> Every stone on the land,
> Each rock and each hill,
> Each fountain and rill,
> Each herb and each tree,
> Mountain, hill, earth and sea,
> Cloud, Meteor and Star
> Are Men seen Afar.[65]

The grain of sand or the wild flower are not only microcosms;
but—as John Beer has expressed it—the state described is that
in which 'a single object can literally become the focus of the
universe, acting symbolically to reveal its coherence and form.
. . . Neither the grain nor the flower acts of itself, however; each
demands the presence of an imagination which is willing both
to see and to receive.'[66]

So the smallest can be, in a sense, the vast; the ridiculous
can become the sublime. It depended—as Coleridge put it—
on the magnifying power of the poet's eye, which is only yet
another way of defining imagination. Sitting sleepily in front

of his fire one night in the summer of 1800, Coleridge scribbled in his notebook:

It is eleven o'clock at night. See that conical volcano of coal, half-an-inch high, ejaculating its inverted cone of smoke—the smoke in what a furious mood—this way, that way, and what a noise!

> The poet's eye in his tipsy hour
> Hath a magnifying power,
> Or rather emancipates his eyes
> Of the accident of size.
> In unctuous cone of kindling coal,
> Or smoke from his pipe's bole
> His eye can see
> Phantoms of sublimity.[67]

This is a classic exposition of early Romantic epistemology—Coleridge's Imagination; Blake's Vision; Schleiermacher's *Gefühl*; Schelling's *Gemüt*; in its more modern guise, Paul Tillich's 'divination'.[68] Its source was unquestionably the Platonic tradition, and its antithesis was deliberately and self-consciously eighteenth-century empiricism in the tradition of Aristotle and Locke.

2

The Vision of the Child

The notion that childhood is a state of grace and that maturity implies declension or a fall is one with which theologians are quite familiar. But when F. D. Maurice observed to Edward Strachey that 'all little children are Platonists', he was making an epistemological statement rather than a theological one. What Lionel Trilling has written of Wordsworth's *Immortality Ode*, that it is a poem 'concerned with ways of seeing and then with ways of knowing',[1] is the clearest guide to Maurice's meaning. He was echoing faithfully Wordsworth's wistful cry— 'the things which I have seen I now can see no more. . . . Whither is fled the visionary gleam? Where is it now, the glory and the dream?'

There is an infant glory which is lost in later life. Words-worth's *Ode* was by no means, as we shall see, the only Romantic poem on this theme, but it is certainly the most celebrated. It is also something of a puzzle because it was written in two parts, with a two-year gap between the fourth and the fifth stanzas, and the mood of the longer addendum is much more optimistic than the opening verses composed in March 1802. There is loss, but there is also gain; and it is quite clear that the message of hope was addressed to Coleridge, whose predica-ment—the loss of his imaginative power—the whole poem seems primarily to concern. In fact the *Immortality Ode* is really a dialogue with Coleridge. The first four verses were written almost immediately after a discussion at Grasmere with Coleridge on childish innocence; the opening lines are a gentle parody of Coleridge's poem *The Mad Monk*, written in 1800; and the 'child' of the poem—'the six years' darling of a pigmy size'—is no hypothetical child. In part he is the boy Words-worth himself, whose sense of the sublime is so superbly

25

captured in the early sections of *The Prelude*; but in part also he is young Hartley Coleridge, to whom Wordsworth had addressed a special sonnet in 1802, on being six years old.

The second part of the *Ode* is Wordsworth's response to Coleridge's *Dejection*, his lament in 1802 on the suspension of 'what nature gave me at my birth, My shaping spirit of Imagination'. Wordsworth recognizes what all men must lose by growing up; but also perceives what one can gain through the development and sharpening of other powers that need not be lost. Thus 'we will grieve not, rather find / Strength in what remains behind'. The *Immortality Ode*—in the words of Sir Maurice Bowra—'is a declaration of belief, intended to counteract the searching doubts and melancholy fears which Wordsworth saw in Coleridge and had felt in a lesser degree in himself'.[2]

Now one can say a great deal more about this fascinating poem; but the other interesting feature of it is that it contains the finest Romantic exposition of the Platonic doctrine of *anamnesis*, as an explanation of the visionary powers of the child:

> Our birth is but a sleep and a forgetting:
> The soul that rises with us, our life's star,
> Hath had elsewhere its setting,
> And cometh from afar;
> Not in entire forgetfulness,
> And not in utter nakedness,
> But trailing clouds of glory do we come
> From God, who is our home.

Wordsworth was himself aware of the ultimate Platonic source of the idea of pre-existence, while non-committal as to the extent of his belief in it. He wrote to Miss Fenwick some years later:

To that dream-like vividness and splendour which invest objects of sight in childhood, everyone, I believe, if he would look back, could bear testimony. . . . I took hold of the notion of pre-existence as having sufficient foundation in humanity for authorizing me to make for my purpose the best use of it I could as a poet.[3]

There is no evidence that Wordsworth ever made a serious study of Plato. Much of his poetry contains what may be described as 'natural' Platonism, but the actual references to Plato are very few indeed, probably no more than five.[4] Although there was an edition of Plato in the Rydal Mount Library,[5] all the Platonism, either implicit or explicit, could have been derived from writers within the tradition rather than from Plato himself. Indeed, in noting that the *Immortality Ode* stands somewhat on its own as a Wordsworth poem—the diction is unusual for one thing—some commentators have observed that the imagery is nearer to Neoplatonism than to Plato. The metaphor of 'sleep' and 'forgetting', for instance, can be found in a passage of Proclus on the pre-existence of the soul; and there is no doubt that Coleridge was familiar with it since this passage was one of several extracts from the early Neoplatonists, compiled by Ficino, in a work which Coleridge purchased from Robson's of New Bond Street in 1796.[6]

Walter Pater has described the *Immortality Ode* as a travesty of Platonism and suggested that Wordsworth drew his imagery from Henry Vaughan's poem, *The Retreat*.[7] It is equally possible, for Coleridge himself noted the affinity, that he had read Henry More's *Song of the Soul*.[8] John Stuart Mill went so far in his criticism of the *Ode* that he maintained that Wordsworth's figure of a sleeping and a forgetting was the absolute opposite of what Plato was intending when he made *anamnesis* the explanation of intuitive perception.[9] At any rate, the general consensus would appear to be that Wordsworth used the Platonic concept in a purely metaphorical sense. In the words of Alec King, the fifth verse of the *Immortality Ode* 'is not in the least like a statement of belief in pre-existence. It is the account of our universal human experience, in terms of myth.'[10]

The curiously unplatonic element in the Romantics' use of the doctrine of pre-existence was their application of it to the perception of the child. Only in one sense could this be considered a justifiable interpretation of Plato's teaching, and this requires some explanation. There are three occasions in the Dialogues when Plato associates the concept of *anamnesis* with pre-existence. In the *Phaedrus* the concept occurs almost as an irrelevance, when Socrates introduces the myth of the winged charioteer and the heavenly procession in order to bring Phaedrus to an understanding of the true nature of love. In the course of this myth, the doctrine of recollection is explained in terms of the soul's return to the body after having a vision of the eternal. While the soul is in the company of God, it grows its wings whereby it will pass again into a human frame. Only the soul of one who has loved truth will be able to grow these wings.[11]

In the *Phaedo* the notion of *anamnesis* is referred to by Cebes as Socrates' 'favourite doctrine'[12] and is mentioned in order to prove the immortality of the soul. In the *Meno*, the immortality of the soul is first advanced in order to prove that knowledge is recollection. Here two points are made: firstly, that recollection involves strenuous activity—'for as all nature is akin, and the soul has learned all things, there is no difficulty in her eliciting, or as men say learning, all out of a single recollection, if a man is strenuous and does not faint'. Secondly, Socrates says that this is the *only* process of knowledge. 'All inquiry and all learning is but recollection', observes Socrates, and he then demonstrates the truth of this by picking on an attendant boy and subjecting him to a test of geometry, purely by asking the right questions.[13]

This could be interpreted as supplying the grounds for Maurice's statement that all children are Platonists. Both in the *Euthydemus*[14] and, more explicitly, in the *Meno*,[15] Socrates is saying that education as understood by the rhetoricians and the sophists is no education at all. The truth, after all, is already there. All that is needed is the art of extracting it. But Socrates does not conclude that a child has a greater knowledge of the truth than a full-grown man. It might be so if one argued that in the infancy of one's life, the soul, newly arrived from its seat of observation within eternity, had a clearer perception of the infinite than it would ever have again while entrapped within the human form. This is a reasonable corollary although Plato never explicitly states it. Indeed, it would seem that Plato had rather a low regard for the perception of the child. In the *Phaedo*, Cebes tells Socrates that whatever a philosopher may feel about the immortality of the soul, the childish, credulous part of our nature makes death to us 'a sort of hobgoblin'.[16] Socrates speaks contemptuously of children in the *Gorgias* as equating pleasure with the good, and refers to a similar misconception amongst 'men who have no more sense than children'.[17] Again, in the *Sophist*, the child is pictured by both Socrates and Theaetetus as likely to be taken in by imitation and is therefore easy prey to painters, magicians, mimics and sophists themselves.[18] It would be contrary to the entire argument of the *Republic* that a child, who might have the philosophic potential or germ within him from the start, could conceivably by-pass the careful training in pure mathematics, music and dialectic which would enable him to gain knowledge of the invisible world.

The concept of the child-philosopher, then, appears to be a form of bastard Platonism, or at least a peculiar whim of the Romantics. Something very similar is certainly found in German Romanticism, significantly enough in the writings of those most profoundly influenced by the Platonic tradition. Friedrich Schlegel in *Lucinde* portrays the child as a prophet and a seer, as does Novalis in an unfinished novel.[19] Goethe's Mignon in *Wilhelm Meister*, the young hermaphrodite, certainly has intuitive vision, while resembling rather Browning's 'Pippa' than Wordsworth's 'six years' darling of a pigmy size'. The idea was sufficiently current for Hegel firmly to attack it in the *Logic*. He interpreted Plato's doctrine of knowledge as recollection in the sense that ideas existed implicitly in man, referring to a potential or capacity and no more.[20] On the alleged wisdom of the child, Hegal wrote in the *Logic* as follows:

The mind is not mere instinct; on the contrary, it essentially involves the tendency to reasoning and meditation. Childlike innocence no doubt has in it something fascinating and attractive; but only because it reminds us of what the spirit must win for itself. The harmoniousness of childhood is a gift from the hands of nature; the second harmony must spring from the labour and culture of the spirit. And so the words of Christ, 'Except ye *become* as little children' etc., are very far from telling us that we must always remain children.[21]

'Except ye become as little children'—one wonders whether this might not be a clue. By the Platonic equation of virtue and knowledge, it might well be reasonable to represent the child as innocent and therefore—in a sense—all wise too. It is interesting to note that in Schleiermacher, in whom the pietistic influence was so strong and had blended in his intellectually formative years with a Romantic Platonism, the child became the archetype of the sublime, the pure and the innocent. Right through his dialogue, *The Christmas Eve*, runs the theme of 'the idealization of childhood and the yearning to be reborn into its innocent serenity'.[22] And in the words of Karoline, describing the child Sofie—who is the focus of the attention of all as the thoughts of the family turn to the Nativity—we find an image of the child's instinctive grasp of the wholeness of things, that sense of the vast which fascinated all the English Romantics, and notably Coleridge and Newman. Sofie, Karoline says, 'has shown us very clearly what the temper of a child is, without which one cannot enter into the kingdom of God; just this— to take every mood and feeling for itself and to want to have it only as unalloyed and whole'.[23]

In Christian thought, especially within the pietistic tradition, there would be an unavoidable collision between such a concept and the Augustinian teaching on Original Sin. But the sentiment could very easily be transferred to the baptismal service, as it appears to have been with Coleridge, who—in spite of his disbelief in Original Sin—regarded the baptismal service as 'almost perfect. . . . None of the services of the Church affect me so much as this. I never could attend a christening without tears bursting forth at the sight of the helpless innocent in a pious clergyman's arms.'[24] Indeed, Coleridge rejected the Church's teaching on Original Sin just because he could not reconcile it with his conviction of natural innocence. There may be an innate corruptible human will which works in a mysterious way, but it cannot be present in an infant since its will is inoperable and therefore incapable of corruption.[25]

The much more likely explanation of this peculiar preoccupation with the child and its union of innocence and intuitive perception was the fact that the Platonism of the Romantics fused with what has been described as the 'cult of sensibility' so closely associated with Rousseau. If Rousseau respected man in the state of nature, he had logically to find the perfect form of man himself in his most natural state—

that is, as an infant entirely free from the world's corruptions;
and in *Emile* he gave expression to that belief with such ex-
travagance and power that it was later acclaimed by Lord
Morley to have been 'one of the seminal books in the history
of literature'.[26] The English Romantics actually employed the
language of *Emile* much less than one might have expected;
but the belief in original innocence and in the testimony of
natural emotions (*je sens, donc je suis*), which had drawn Rousseau into the cult of sensibility, worked equally powerfully
upon them to convince them of the exalted nature of a child's
perception and the deleterious effects of insensitive and formal
education.

It must be loss to a child, so Wordsworth thought, to confine
him to the shades of the prison house, when in earlier days of
happy spontaneity he had blown 'mimic hootings to the silent
owls'.[27] Blake was even more emphatic, and brought Plato
into his condemnation. 'There *is* no use in education', he once
said to Crabb Robinson. 'I hold it to be wrong. It is the great
sin. It is eating of the tree of knowledge of good and evil.
This was the fault of Plato. He knew nothing but the virtues
and vices, and good and evil. There is nothing in all that.
Everything is good in God's eyes.'[28] Coleridge would not have
gone nearly so far as that. In considering the nature of knowledge, he assures us in *Aids to Reflection*, we must all be as humble
as children for they have the truest sense of *credo ut intelligam*.[29]
But children cannot be left entirely to themselves to acquire
their own values. In the *Table Talk* he recalled a conversation
he had had on this subject with John Thelwall.

Thelwall thought it very unfair to influence a child's mind by inculcating any opinions before it should have come to years of discretion and be able to choose for itself. I showed him my garden and
told him it was my botanical garden. 'How so?', said he, 'it is
covered with weeds'.

'Oh!', I replied, 'that is only because it has not yet come to the
age of discretion and choice. The weeds, you see, have taken the
liberty to grow and I thought it unfair in me to prejudice the soil
towards roses and strawberries'.[30]

What the Romantics all appear to have had in common
was the belief that it was criminal to stifle a child's innate

imaginative sense. For the child was the poet in embryo. Its sense of wonder, its capacity to marvel, and—above all—its recognition of the wholeness of things, or its intuitive perception of the one behind the many, must be nourished by stories or tales which stimulated the imagination to further flights. Fantasy was preferable to fact. In a superb autobiographical letter to Thomas Poole in October 1797, Coleridge explained why this was so:

Should children be permitted to read Romances, and Relations of Giants and Magicians, and Genii?—I know all that has been said against it, but I have formed my faith in the affirmative—I know no other way of giving the mind a love of 'the Great', and 'the Whole'— Those who have been led to the same truths step by step thro' the constant testimony of their senses, seem to me to want a sense which I possess—They contemplate nothing but *parts*—and all *parts* are necessarily little—and the Universe to them is but a mass of *little things*. . . . I have known some who have been *rationally* educated, as it is styled. They were marked by a microscopic acuteness; but when they looked at great things, all became a blank and they saw nothing—and denied (very illogically) that anything could be seen; and uniformly put the negation of a power for the possession of a power—and called the want of imagination Judgment, and the never being moved to Rapture Philosophy![31]

Certainly this was Coleridge's own experience. In a letter to Poole, written five days earlier, he had described his reading as a child of Tom Hickathrift and Jack the Giantkiller, and how he would then leap about the churchyard to act out what he had read; and then—at the age of six—when he encountered *Robinson Crusoe* and the *Arabian Nights*, the fascination had so gripped him that his eyes would be for ever straying to the window-sill where the books were kept. His father, believing that this preoccupation with romances was unhealthy and introspective, burnt the books, but the effect could not so easily be eradicated. 'I became a *dreamer*', he told Poole;[32] and to John Thelwall he explained what this meant to his mind. 'My mind feels as if it ached to behold and know something *great*—something *one* and *indivisible*.'[33]

It is interesting to observe that with John Henry Newman a similar experience had a very similar effect. 'I used to wish the Arabian Tales were true', he wrote; 'my imagination ran on unknown influences, on magical powers, and talismans. . . . I thought life might be a dream, or I an Angel, and all this world a deception, my fellow-angels by a playful device concealing themselves from me, and deceiving me with the semblance of a material world.'[34] Later, in a brilliant essay, Newman distinguished between the poetic sense of the child and the scientific mind which comes with advancing years.

Poetry does not address the reason, but the imagination and affections; it leads to admiration, enthusiasm, devotion, love. The vague, the uncertain, the irregular, the sudden, are among its attributes and sources. Hence it is that a child's mind is so full of poetry because he knows so little; and an old man of the world so devoid of poetry, because his experience of facts is so wide. Hence it is that nature is commonly more poetical than art, in spite of Lord Byron, because it is less comprehensible and less patient of definitions; history more poetical than philosophy; the savage than the citizen; the knight-errant than the brigadier-general; the winding bridle-path than the straight railroad; the sailing vessel than the steamer; the ruin than the spruce suburban box; the Turkish robe or Spanish doublet than the French dresscoat.[35]

We may grant that distinctions of measure and discernment of categories are important to the imaginative poet as well as to the scientist. Just because he has them, the poet is a philosopher in a sense that a child can never be. Coleridge recognized this in his careful analysis of the loosing and binding power of the imagination, as we have seen, and his approval of the statement of H. S. Reimarus that 'we have no conception, not even of single objects, except by means of the similarity we perceive between them and other objects'.[36] F. D. Maurice, likewise, pointed to the inability of a child to make refined distinctions, arising from the infant state when all men are called 'father' and all women 'mother'.[37] But the particular genius of the child—and to Coleridge a child possesses genius rather than talent[38]—was the combination of simplicity, innocence and sensibility which enabled it to penetrate to the essence of what it observed, without being able to explain the process in intellectual or rational terms.

It was this faculty that could so easily be lost through education; which fantasy and romance might keep alive, while fact and scientific explanation could so easily stifle. Feed him on Jack the Giantkiller and the *Arabian Nights* and keep Newton long at bay. Or, as Wordsworth put it in the *Prelude,* subscribing to this sentiment with all his heart—

> Oh! give us once again the Wishing-Cap
> Of Fortunatus, and the invisible coat
> Of Jack the Giant-killer, Robin Hood,
> And Sabra in the forest with St George![39]

None felt this more keenly than William Blake. The curse of schooling—to Blake—was that too often 'the tender plants are strip'd / Of their joy in the springing day!'[40] The roles of teacher and pupil should be reversed. It is the child who sees and the adult who has become blind. Blake told John Trusler, who had found so many of Blake's visions unintelligible, that he ought to look for assistance from a child. These visions 'have been elucidated by children, who have taken a greater delight in contemplating my pictures, than I even hoped. . . . Some children are fools and so are some old men. But there is a vast majority on the side of Imagination or Spiritual Sensation.'[41] Fairy-tales feed the visionary power. Thus Blake used the symbol of 'fairies and elves' to represent the creative energies; and it is in this sense that Blake's motto for the *Songs of Innocence and Experience* should be read:

> The Good are attracted by Men's perceptions,
> And think not for themselves;
> Till Experience teaches them to catch
> And to cage the Fairies and Elves.[42]

As for *anamnesis,* Blake accepted the doctrine without question. 'Reynolds thinks that Man learns all that he knows', he wrote on one occasion. 'I say on the Contrary that Man Brings All that he has or can have Into the World with him. Man is Born like a Garden ready Planted and Sown. This World is too poor to produce one Seed.'[43] Expressed in verse in a letter to Thomas Butts, this becomes:

The Vision of the Child

I remain'd as a Child;
All I ever had known
Before me bright shone.[44]

Blake absorbed this idea from his reading within the Platonic tradition, reinforced by his friendship with Thomas Taylor, who also had no difficulties about accepting it.[45] But Blake does not appear to have transmitted the concept to the other Romantics. Shelley, for instance, made the discovery himself on reading the *Phaedo* through Floyer Sydenham's translation; and it possessed him utterly at once. He interpreted it immediately as endowing infants with a unique insight into the eternal order. His friend, T. J. Hogg, pictured him pacing his room, shaking his long, wild locks and discoursing in solemn fashion on the consequences of this great truth. 'Every true Platonist, he used to say, must be a lover of children, for they are our masters and instructors in philosophy.'[46] Once, while walking with Hogg over Magdalen Bridge, Shelley encountered a woman bustling across with a child in her arms. He stopped, advanced on the woman, and 'with abrupt dexterity he caught hold of the child'. There was a bit of a struggle because the woman feared that Shelley intended her child an injury. But not so—

'Will your baby tell us anything about pre-existence, madam?' he asked in a piercing voice, and with a wistful look.

The mother made no answer, but perceiving that Shelley's object was not murderous, but altogether harmless, she dismissed her apprehensions, and relaxed her hold.

'Will your baby tell us anything about pre-existence, madam?' he repeated with unabated earnestness.

'He cannot speak, Sir', said the mother seriously.

'Worse and worse', cried Shelley, with an air of deep disappointment, shaking his long hair most pathetically about his young face, 'but surely the babe can speak if he will, for he is only a few weeks' old. He may fancy perhaps that he cannot, but it is only a silly whim; he cannot have forgotten entirely the use of speech in so short a time, the thing is absolutely impossible.'

'It is not for me to dispute with you, gentlemen', the woman meekly replied, her eye glancing at our academical garb, 'but I can safely declare that I never heard him speak, nor any child, indeed of his age.'

35

... Shelley pressed his (the baby's) fat cheek with his finger, ... the mother was permitted to proceed. ... Shelley sighed as we walked on. 'How provokingly close are these new-born babes! ... but it is not the less certain, notwithstanding the cunning attempts to conceal the truth, that all knowledge is reminiscence.'[47]

Neither Coleridge nor Wordsworth learnt the idea of *anamnesis* as applied to childish perception from Blake. Wordsworth only knew of Blake's writings through his friendship with Crabb Robinson. Although four of Blake's lyrics appear in his commonplace book for either 1802 or 1804 (in Dorothy Wordsworth's hand),[48] he does not seem to have read the *Songs of Innocence and Experience* until May 1812.[49] From a letter to C. A. Tulk, dated 12 February 1818, it appears that Coleridge's first acquaintance with them was not until nearly six years later.[50] In any case, they both differed from Blake and Shelley in the degree of their commitment to the idea. Wordsworth's use of it was not confined to the *Immortality Ode*. There is a suggestion of it in his poem 'To H. C. Six Years Old', written in 1802, and a much more explicit reference in Book II of the *Prelude*:

> but that the soul,
> Remembering how she felt, but what she felt
> Remembering not, retains an obscure sense
> Of possible sublimity.[51]

Coleridge employed it in the sonnet on the birth of Hartley Coleridge in 1797 ('and some have said, we liv'd, ere yet this robe of flesh we wore'), ascribing the notion to the followers of Fénélon.[52] In the *Destiny of Nations*, *anamnesis* is linked with a clear reference to the allegory of the Cave in the *Republic*:

> For all that meets the bodily sense I deem
> Symbolical, one mighty alphabet
> For infant minds: and we in this low world
> Placed with our back to bright Reality,
> That we may learn with young unwounded ken
> The substance from its shadow.[53]

Wordsworth, as we have seen, admitted that he used Plato's teaching on pre-existence metaphorically. It may well be that Coleridge would have gone no further than this. But the fact remains that his remarks on pre-existence are bewilderingly inconsistent. He attacked Wordsworth vehemently in the second volume of the *Biographia Literaria* for his language in the *Ode*, although he profoundly admired the poem, as is clear from a reference in *The Friend*,[54] and singled out—as a private comment—the delicacy with which Wordsworth had treated the theme of pre-existence.[55] At one moment he could write:

In what sense is a child of that age (six years old) a *philosopher*? In what sense does he *read* 'the eternal deep'? In what sense is he declared to be '*for ever haunted*' by the Supreme Being? or so inspired as to deserve the splendid title of a *mighty prophet*, or *blessed seer*? By reflection? by knowledge? by conscious intuition? or by *any* form or modification of consciousness? These would be tidings indeed. . . . Children of this age give us no such information of themselves.[56]

Such nonsense is this that Coleridge supposes that no one for a moment could take Wordsworth seriously. They would be as little disposed to charge him with that as they would be to hold that Plato himself 'ever meant or taught it'.[57] But it is a different story in the *Notebooks*:

To deduce instincts from obscure recollections of a pre-existent state—I have often thought of it—Ey! have I said, when I have seen certain tempers and actions in Hartley, that is I in my future state/ so I think often times that my children are my soul.[58]

It was when Coleridge looked at his son Hartley that he wondered more and more about the curious perception of the child. And well he might have done, for Hartley was—to say the least—a very unusual boy; offspring, of course, of a very unusual father. A surfeit of the *Arabian Nights* had made Coleridge dreamy and introspective, contemptuous of the rough games and philistine attitudes of his contemporaries. He was precocious; as a Grecian at Christ's Hospital looked upon with awe as he discoursed on Plotinus and Iamblichus; he endeared himself to old ladies, relapsed into moods and sometimes erupted into fits of tempestuous anger, as when he flung himself at his older brother Frank with a carving knife, because the boy had taunted him for an over-scrupulous attention to the texture of a slice of cheese.[59]

Like father, like son. Of all Coleridge's children, Hartley

was most manifestly the son of his father. All parents delight in the quaintness of their children's observations and reflections, and Coleridge was no exception. Indeed he came increasingly to feel, as he studied Hartley's ways, that the deepest truths were vouchsafed not so much through book-learning but 'by reflecting on my own Being and Observation of the Ways of those about me, especially of little children'.[60] Hartley certainly had a genius for putting difficult concepts into words. 'I am always thinking of my thoughts', he once told his father.[61] Watching with fascination Coleridge writing Greek, he offered the suggestion that they were 'English letters dried up'.[62] At the age of five, on being addressed by the name 'Hartley', the boy looked up and asked 'Which Hartley?'

'Why is there more than one Hartley?' (Crabb Robinson recorded the event).

'Yes, there's a deal of Hartleys.'

'How so?'

'There's Picture Hartley (Hazlitt had painted a portrait of him), and Shadow Hartley, and there's Echo Hartley, and there's Catch-me-fast Hartley,'—at the same time seizing his own arm with the other hand very eagerly, an action which shows his mind must have been led to reflect on what Kant called the great and inexplicable mystery that man should be both his own subject and object, and that these should yet be one.[63]

Crabb Robinson may have elaborated this somewhat. The incident is not quite as Coleridge described it to Dorothy Wordsworth at the time.[64] It is possible, too, that Coleridge, who was making his first study of Kant during this period, introduced this concept to his children, with whom he quite obviously held a somewhat adult discourse. It is significant that two years later, little Derwent Coleridge appears to have made a similar discovery—that there were at least two Derwents, himself and his reflection.[65] This should not, however, detract from Hartley's undoubted sensitivity to deep philosophical concepts. 'A strange, strange Boy', Coleridge commented in 1803. 'Exquisitely wild! An utter Visionary! Like Moon among thin Clouds, he moves in a circle of Light of his own making—he alone, in a Light of his own.'[66]

'Hartley Coleridge', wrote Walter Bagehot in a charming

essay, 'was not like the Duke of Wellington.'[67] That was his trouble. He had no organization; his fatal precocity betokened a mind so hopelessly introspective that he never came to terms with the world. 'As often happens, being very little of a boy in actual childhood, Hartley preserved into manhood and age all of boyhood which he ever possessed—its beaming imagination and its wayward will.'[68] He maintained also his fantastic aptitude for talking about his thoughts. This, after all, was the essence of his strangeness. The sensations which he felt as a child were not all that uncommon, and what is striking about the boy's remarks is the uncanny way in which they evoke dimly-remembered questionings about oneself and the world either from one's own early wrestlings over a primitive epistemology, or from what one has observed in others at that stage of life.

Perhaps the child is, indeed, a poet in embryo. Wordsworth admitted, in commenting upon the *Immortality Ode*, that 'I was often unable to think of external things as having external existence, and I communed with all that I saw as something not apart from, but inherent in, my own immaterial nature.'[69] Bonamy Price recalled meeting Wordsworth as an old man and asking him exactly what he meant by this remark.

The remarkable old man raised his aged form erect; he was walking in the middle, and passed across me to a five-barred gate in the wall which bounded the road on the side of the lake. He clenched the top bar firmly with his right hand, pushed strongly against it, and then uttered these ever-memorable words:

'There was a time in my life when I had to push against something that resisted to be sure that there was anything outside me. I was sure of my own mind; everything else fell away and vanished into thought.'[70]

A little while back, we noted Newman saying almost the same thing. The child, being so unselfconsciously self-conscious (if one may put it that way), regards himself as the focal point of the world, and sees a harmony perhaps of his own devising. In the words of Edwin Muir, he has 'a picture of human existence peculiar to himself, which he probably never remembers after he has lost it'.[71] Could it be the original vision of

the world? Who can tell? If there be a God, it may be reasonable to suppose that there is a harmony which He can perceive. And perhaps the child intuitively grasps this harmony,
thereby experiencing a glimmering of that process of divination for which Romantic poets and theologians have so earnestly
craved. This may not be what Plato actually meant by *anamnesis*, but it still may be not so very far from the truth.

3

Opposites and Contraries

The implications of F. D. Maurice's remark that 'all little children are Platonists' have now been examined. The next question should logically be—what did Maurice himself understand by Platonism, which he so clearly preferred to the rival philosophical tradition? Fortunately Maurice himself was very explicit here and has left on record his own estimation of the peculiar genius of Plato and the most important truth which the Platonic tradition has sought to safeguard.

He tells us, for instance, that his introduction to Plato came through Julius Hare at Trinity College, Cambridge, and that it was from Hare's lectures on the *Gorgias* that he came to see that the essence of Plato's teaching was that 'there was a way out of party opinions, which is not a compromise between them, but which is implied in both, and of which each is bearing witness'. He goes on: 'Hare did not tell us this. . . . Plato himself does not say it; he makes us feel it.' From this revelation, through Hare's lectures, 'I can trace the most permanent effect on my character, and on all my modes of contemplating subjects, natural, human, and divine.'[1]

That is the simple answer. But to explain what it means, whether it is a faithful interpretation of the Platonic tradition or not, how it came to be a leading idea within nineteenth-century Romanticism, especially in Coleridge, is a much more complex task. For this is none other than the concept of *coincidentia oppositorum*, the reconciliation of opposites, the notion that truth lies at both extremes but never in the middle, which is the key to a true understanding of Romantic philosophy, without which the writings of Blake, Coleridge, Schelling, Hegel, and—for that matter—Maurice himself, are almost totally unintelligible.

Our enquiry should attempt to answer four questions: what are its Platonic roots? Why did the Romantics seize upon it as the universal law? How did it take shape in their own thought? Finally, what were its philosophical and theological implications?

The Romantics had posed a very Greek question: could they find the One behind the many? Could they identify the universal law whereby the deepest truths were discernible? Not unnaturally, they examined the Greek answers to that question; and—sooner or later—they were bound to encounter the very first answers of the Pythagorean and Eleatic schools, notably Heraclitus, Parmenides and Zeno. In Heraclitus they found the first enunciation of a dynamic principle in the form of reconciliation theory—the notion of the universe as being in a state of constant tension between two poles, so that the unity which all men sought could only be expressed in terms of the synthesis of the opposing poles. In 1817, in a letter to the Swedenborgian C. A. Tulk, Coleridge described his quest for this universal law as follows:

Accept this very rude sketch of the many rudiments of *Heraclitus redivivus.* .... I found it during the study of Plato, and the scholar of Ammonias, and in later times of Scotus ... Giordano Bruno, Behmen, and the much calumniated Spinoza ... long before Schelling had published his first and imperfect view.[2]

In *The Friend*, he announced with a didactic flourish both the universal law and its lineage:

EVERY POWER IN NATURE AND IN SPIRIT *must evoke an opposite as the sole means of condition of its manifestation*: AND ALL OPPOSITION IS A TENDENCY TO RE-UNION. This is the universal law of Polarity—of essential Dualism, first promulgated by Heraclitus, 2000 years afterwards republished, and made the foundation both of Logic, of Physics and of Metaphysics by Giordano Bruno.[3]

It may be noted that Coleridge is more confident than F. D. Maurice in identifying the Platonic roots. 'I found it during the study of Plato' he writes. Maurice will only say 'Plato himself does not say it; he makes us feel it.' In the end, we may come to the conclusion that Maurice was the more exact. Plato was for ever worrying over the Heraclitean law of

42

dynamism and the paradoxes posed by Parmenides and Zeno. In none of the four dialogues in which the matter is discussed— *Parmenides*, the *Sophist*, the *Philebus* and *Theaetetus*—is it at all clear what Plato's own views were, a situation aggravated by the dialogue form. Socrates himself, in his modesty and ex- aggerated respect for the masters of the Eleatic school, is not always very clear either. In the *Theaetetus* he gives an unusually lengthy discourse on the 'charming speculations' of Heraclitus in a tone suggestive of irony,[4] but when Theodorus asks in good-natured exasperation 'I should like to know, Socrates, by heaven I should, whether you mean to say that all this is un- true', he receives a characteristically evasive answer.[5] There is no doubt that Socrates occasionally mocks the notion that all opposition can be reconciled. In the *Euthydemus*, for instance, he presents a parody of the argument that existence and non- existence are in reality the same;[6] he jokes about Theaetetus' use of the phrase 'truly false';[7] but it is never quite clear whether Socrates intends to go so far as to mock the master rather than to expose the extravagances of his disciples.

At one moment Socrates can expatiate on the curious para- dox that 'extremes meet', pointing out to Protagoras that 'the most extreme opposites have some qualities in common' and that 'white is in a certain way like black, and hard is like soft',[8] and yet he answers Protarchus in the *Philebus* that he must never rely on this argument because 'we all know that black is not only unlike, but even deliberately opposed to white'.[9] He is fascinated by the relationship between 'Being' and 'Becoming', discussing with Protarchus the paradoxes of Simonides,[10] and goes so far as to say in the *Phaedo* that 'all things which have opposites' are 'generated out of their oppo- sites';[11] and then—in the same dialogue—qualifies this by pointing out that certain 'essential opposites' can never be reconciled, that fire cannot be cold, and odd can never be even.[12]

Plato's contribution to reconciliation theory would appear to be fourfold. Firstly, he familiarized his posterity with the nature of the Heraclitean and Eleatic debates. Secondly, by his use of the tool of dialectic, he made a clear distinction between opposites or contraries and contradictions. The Socratic method—as is well known—is a process whereby opinions about abstract truths are forced by the posing of the right questions into a contradiction. Argument therefore proceeds by a succession of blind alleys. A definition is put to the test until a contradiction proves it untenable. When a definition is finally made that avoids outright contradiction, then at last the road becomes clear. Sometimes (as in the *Parmenides*) it never does, because every route taken appears to be a *cul-de-sac* and every dialectical study ends in a contradiction. And this is failure; and is admitted as such. If Plato had really taught that truth was a union of contradictions, he would have been exposing to ridicule and ultimate rejection the whole foundation of his intellectual system.

Most Platonists have followed him here. Even the wild and idiosyncratic Blake saw a fundamental distinction between 'contraries' (which were the necessary condition of all progression) and 'negations' which were incapable of generating anything. Coleridge was both more explicit and more philosophical. His distinction was between 'opposites' which are polar positions tending to reunion, and 'contraries' which are logical monstrosities and outright contradictions. 'Antagonist forces are necessarily of the same kind', he wrote in the *Constitution of the Church and State*. '*Inter res heterogeneas non datur oppositio*; that is, contraries cannot be opposites. Alike in the primary and the metaphorical use of the word, rivals (*rivales*) are those only who inhabit the opposite banks of the same stream.'*13

Thirdly, Plato's theory of ideas posited a noumenal world beyond the world of phenomena which could be penetrated by the cultivation of the art of dialectic. This was not only in itself a form of reconciliation theory on the Pythagorean pattern—by conceiving of the universe as embracing the two poles of the static infinite order and the dynamic finite world of motion; it also provided an explanation for some ultimate reconciliation of opposites in the real world of universals, where problems which baffled human minds (such as the four antinomies of Kant) would be enlightened by some higher reason which would dispel the discordances and conflicts of the world

* This point is elaborated in Appendix B.

of shadows in which we live. It was the development of this
Platonic concept, especially by Bruno and Boehme, that the
Romantics cherished most. All opposites are ultimately synthe-
sized in God. This, for instance, is Coleridge in his marginalia
to Boehme's *Aurora*:

By quality Behmen intends that act of each elementary Power, by
which it energizes in its peculiar kind. But in the Deity is an absolute
synthesis of opposites. Plato in Parmenide and Giordano Bruno
passim have spoken many things well on this awful mystery—the
latter more clearly.[14]

In this respect the Neoplatonists, and especially the Renaissance and seventeenth-century Platonists, rendered explicit
what in Plato had only been implicit.

This is particularly noticeable in the fourth (and final) aspect
of Plato's treatment of the reconciliation theme—his androgynous imagery, borrowed by his followers from the speech of
Aristophanes in the *Symposium*, a passage which is in no way
central to the argument of the dialogue. Aristophanes, who
had been thwarted in his earlier attempts to discourse on love
by an untimely attack of hiccoughs, at last is able to get a word
in and presents his own theory in the form of an account of the
origin of the human race. At the beginning of the world, there
were three sexes not two—man, woman, and the union of the
two. 'The primeval man was round, and had four hands and
four feet, back and sides forming a circle, one head with two
faces, looking opposite ways, set on a round neck and precisely
alike.' Grotesque creatures they were indeed—very quick, for
instance, because they whizzed about like balls; terrible too,
because they had illusions of grandeur and dared to attack the
Gods. Zeus, however, was not discountenanced. He punished
these hideous hermaphrodites by cutting them in two 'like a
sorb-apple which is halved for pickling, or as you might divide
an egg with a hair'; carried out a few appropriate adjustments
to their private parts, and left them to wander mournfully in
search of their other halves.[15]

So human beings had once been androgynous. Since God
had separated the male and female elements, two opposite
forces, represented as active and passive, and indispensable to

each other for continuity, were striving for reunion. Was not this some allegory of a universal law, some secret explanation, some *gnosis*, of the dynamic principle constantly at work? Providing a rich source of imagery for literature, it supplied also the key to magic, mysticism and metaphysics. And if more cultivated minds in modern times should think this to be the most monstrous red herring that ever diverted the attentions of seemingly intelligent men, then they should pause before dismissing it with a contemptuous wave. For even if Aristophanes had never recovered from his hiccoughs, the idea (less graphically presented perhaps) would have been encountered elsewhere. It is found in the *Cabbala* as well; and the importance of Bruno, Paracelsus and Boehme (and also the Romantics of the late eighteenth century who read them so avidly) was that they fused Platonism, Neoplatonism and the occult wisdom of the East into a single corpus of esoteric thought,[16] and did so —moreover—with an irrefutable logic. After all, once you accept that there is a universal law, you may safely presume that it has been universally revealed. This was the best excuse possible for extracting truth from a rag-bag, because every science and honest enquiry, however quaint or archaic, must be a reaching-out for the demonstration of that single, universal truth.

At first sight, Blake's sources seem something of a rag-bag. He was for ever using androgynous symbols, the chief of which was Albion, described by Milton Percival as 'the last of a long line of primordial cosmic figures with which the platonizing imagination filled ancient speculation and which came down along esoteric by-paths through the Middle Ages and emerged again into the main highway of knowledge in the Grand Man of Swedenborg'.[17] It would appear that within this mystical tradition, nature abhors duality as much as she abhors a vacuum. Duality may be a fact of existence, but the movement within the universe is always towards the fusion of the two opposite elements into a unity. The distinction might be between mind and will, as with Swedenborg, or between mind and sense in Philo, the Creator and the creature in St Paul, the hidden and the manifest within the Gnostic system of Simon Magus, intellect and will in Paracelsus, the light and the

dark in the *Cabbala*, tincture and substantiality in Boehme—
but all are active and passive elements, represented as polar
opposites in continual tension.[18] So at least it is within the
world of phenomena. The higher realm (and the Platonic
imagery is plain enough here) is a state of undifferentiation,
where the lost is found and the divided are reconciled. As
Boehme put it:

Every essence consisted of two essences, viz. of an inward and an
outward, one seeketh and findeth the other; the outward is nature,
the inward is spirit above nature; and yet there is no separation, but
in that which is included in a time.[19]

This brings us to the second of our four questions. Why,
then, did the Romantics seize upon the idea of the reconciliation of opposites as the universal law for which they were
seeking? The simple answer is that this is what they found in
the books that they were reading. Blake studied Boehme and
Swedenborg, Coleridge was studying the *Aurora* at Christ's
Hospital, later turning to Paracelsus and Henry More's *Con-
iectura Cabbalistica*. Their poetry is full of occult, alchemical and
androgynous images. Everywhere they looked, in seeking to
escape from the Lockean system which they knew to be false,
they found the same answer. Berkeley was infinitely preferable
to Locke; and here again they discovered that the dynamism of
the universe sprang from the tension of polar opposites. The
celebrated metaphysical distinction between *natura naturata* and
natura naturans appeared in Berkeley as part of a fourfold
allegory, the others being Isis and Osiris, the female and the
male, the moon and the sun.[20] The science of alchemy, which
fascinated all the Romantics, testified to the same truth. To the
alchemist, the philosopher's stone was an androgyne. Basil
Valentine actually described it as an hermaphrodite; Starkey
says of the stone that 'it was a reconciliation of Contraries, a
making friendship between enemies'.[21] The process of manu-
facturing the stone was in every detail related to the union of
male and female elements—the intercourse between fire and
mercury, a gestation period of forty weeks, the issue (the stone
itself) becoming self-reproductive, being both the seed of gold
and the seminal product. Other qualities it would have, too—

notably roundness (to symbolize perfection and eternity), and redness (some would have it purple) to satisfy the requirements of colour-symbolism.[22]

Coleridge did not take the alchemists entirely seriously, but at least saw that they arrived at a fundamental truth, only to be diverted into a futile quest for precious metals. 'Alchemy is the theoretic end of chemistry', he wrote in 1832; 'there must be a common law, upon which all can become each, and each all; but then the idea was turned to the coining of gold and silver.'[23]

There must be a common law. In Germany, Goethe, and in England, Coleridge, each applied their polymathic minds to demonstrating it. So Goethe carried out experiments with the physiognomy of the human jaw, set up a microscope and herbarium to study the nature of seeds, experimented with optics to disprove Newton's theory of colours, carried out research on the nature of granite and the formation and transformation of clouds. Coleridge, likewise, yearned to be a chemist, planned to set up a small laboratory at Keswick with Humphrey Davy, dashed off to watch exhibitions of mesmerism, walked the London hospitals with his brother Luke, and speculated on optics, mathematics, physics and the nascent electrical sciences. One day he might be diverted from his tasks by a new train of thought arising from the sight of his urine in a pot; the next he would be moved so vigorously to rub the back of a cat (in order to see the sparks in the dark) that he got badly scratched for his pains.[24] What did it matter? It was all in the interests of the fundamental science.

Now if you know what you are looking for, you are pretty sure to find it. Both Coleridge and Goethe knew from their reading into ancient wisdom what the universal law ought to be and sought confirmation of it from the studies on which they separately engaged. Goethe studied botany in order to find the *Urpflanze*, the primal plant. In his investigations into optics, he experimented with a prism in order to find the spectral colours. To his delight he found that the spectral colours appeared only when both light and shadow (two polar forces) were present. If the opposition was not in evidence, the result was blankness. So the universal law of polarity had been vindicated.[25] It is interesting to observe that Coleridge conducted a very similar experiment to arrive at a very similar conclusion, which he demonstrated as an example of polar opposites in the form of a logical heptad.

The word 'polarity' is the real key to the answer of this, our second question. Coleridge, Goethe, Hegel and Schelling were all convinced that science was on the threshold of the most important 'break-through' which would establish beyond any shadow of doubt that the law of polar opposites, going far back to Heraclitus and the wisdom of the East, was the one fundamental law of the universe, from which all dynamism sprang and through which unity was achieved. And for good reason. They lived through an age which witnessed an astounding development in the field of electrical sciences, most notably the discovery of electricity by Volta and Laplace in 1798. 'A new light had been struck,' Coleridge wrote in a review of the scientific discoveries of modern times, 'a new object of pursuit disclosed, by the discoveries in electricity; and it would be no gross exaggeration to say that the whole frame of natural philosophy was soon adjusted to electrical theories and electrical hypotheses.'[26]

It is given to few men to be able so accurately to account for their own philosophical language and that of their own generation. There can be no doubt that Coleridge was right. With a greater confidence, he advanced a fuller definition of his universal law:

To the twin counterforces of the Magnetic Power, the equilibrium of which is revealed in magnetic Iron, as the substantial, add the twin counterforces, or + and − poles, of the Electrical Powers, the indifference of which is realised in Water, as the Superficial. . . . and you will hear the voice of infant Nature; i.e. you will understand the rudimental products of elementary Powers and Constructions of the phenomenal world. An Enigma not unworthy of Orpheus, and therefore not improbably ascribed to him. . . .

P.S. − and + Magn. Attraction and Repulsion; or Cohesion and Dispersion. − and + Elect. = Contraction and Dilation.[27]

There are many other examples of this language in Coleridge's writings which could be cited, notably in *The Friend*.[28]

But for corroboratory material, both Schelling and Hegel supply the same confidence that contemporary researches into the electrical sciences provide an unchallengeable proof that the reconciliation of opposites is the universal law. Crabb Robinson attended Schelling's lectures at Jena, when he prophesied the demonstration of the interrelation of the several sciences which was soon to come. 'We are accustomed to consider magnetism, electricity and galvanism three distinct sciences', Schelling said. 'And in a certain sense they are. . . . But, in truth, the magnetic, electric, and galvanic powers are only various forms of the same thing; and before many years have elapsed some experimental naturalist will come forward and exhibit visible proofs of this fact.'[29] Not long indeed, as Crabb Robinson lived to see. In 1812 Oersted published his first researches on the identity of chemical and electrical forces, and by 1819 he had found the connecting link between magnetism and electricity, so looking forward to the dramatic advances of Faraday in the 1830's.

Was this, then, the 'break-through'? Hegel certainly thought so. In the *Logic*, he argued the identity of positive and negative on the following grounds:

Positive and Negative are supposed to express an absolute difference. The two however are at bottom the same; the name of either might be transferred to the other. Thus, for example, debts and assets are not two particulars, self-subsisting species of property. What is negative to the debtor, is positive to the creditor. A way to the East is also a way to the West. Positive and negative are therefore intrinsically conditioned by one another, and are only in relation to each other. The north pole of the magnet cannot be without the south pole, and *vice-versa*. If we cut a magnet in two, we have not a north pole in one piece, and a south pole in the other. Similarly in electricity, the positive and the negative are not two diverse and independent fluids. In opposition, the different is not confronted by any other, but by *its* other.[30]

To Hegel, this was fundamental. He puts the point thus: 'In modern physical sciences the opposition, first observed to exist in magnetism as polarity, has come to be regarded as a universal law pervading the whole of nature.'[31]

Now, to the third question. How did this idea of the universal law of polarity take shape in the thought of the Romantics? At a certain level, it might seem to be a piece of mystical or metaphysical nonsense, as parodied in the following limerick, which appeared some years ago in the *New Statesman,* ascribing the idea of *coincidentia oppositorum* to the Chinese doctrine of Tao.

> Said an erudite sinologue, 'How
> Shall I try to explain to you Tao?
> It is Yes; it is No;
> It is stop; it is go;
> But it's neither; do you understand now?'[32]

The two Romantic writers in whom the idea is chiefly found—indeed it is the very basis of their thought—are William Blake and Coleridge. It is the underlying theme of the Lambeth books, in that Blake presents all conflict as arising from the separation of male and female through the division of the original androgyne. The reference to the *Symposium* is obvious. Los was originally an androgyne. In *Urizen* we are told:

> All Eternity shuddered at sight
> Of the first female now separated
> Pale as a cloud of snow
> Waving before the face of Los.[33]

In the *Marriage of Heaven and Hell,* the title itself indicates the polar opposites, the contraries, which have to co-exist, along with Energy and Imagination (symbolized in Orc and Los) and Innocence and Experience, together making the three great Contraries which are the necessary condition of dynamism. 'Without Contraries is no Progression', Blake writes. 'Attraction and Repulsion, Reason and Energy, Love and Hate are necessary to Human Existence.'[34] It is interesting to note that Hell is one of the essential poles. Blake's real Hell, in the sense of the principle of death and inertness is ULRO, which is a negation, not a contrary. In this respect, Blake differed from Swedenborg, and consciously so, since the *Marriage of Heaven and Hell* was written to signify his deviation from orthodox Swedenborgianism. Swedenborg taught that there was 'one family of contraries', meaning that the principle of *coincidentia oppositorum* was the condition of equilibrium. To Blake, the tension between the two poles was the necessary condition of movement and progression.[35]

In Coleridge, the idea took shape chiefly in two forms. The first he called 'trichotomous logic' or 'trichotomy', the principle of which was derived from Bruno and the method from Richard Baxter, the seventeenth-century divine. This was basically a triadic figure—the two poles of thesis and antithesis and a 'higher third' which was the identity of the two. His writing on this subject is so complex, and his application of it, in series of triads, heptads and pentads based on the Pythagorean *tetractys*, so involved, that the exposition of this theme has been reserved to a technical appendix.* This is not to underrate its importance, however. Armed with the technical equipment to apply the law of polarity, Coleridge employed it in every branch of knowledge to which he turned his mind in his later years, but especially philosophy and theology. The *Confessions of an Inquiring Spirit* opens with a pentad of 'operative Christianity'; the *Aids to Reflection* and the *Lay Sermons* are studded with trichotomous arguments. Above all, it was the method by which Coleridge satisfied himself on the truths of orthodox Christian doctrine, and most especially the doctrine of the Trinity.

The second form of expressing the idea of *coincidentia oppositorum* in Coleridge was through the adage 'extremes meet'. This is sometimes expressed in the form of an Aristotelian triad, whereby virtue is represented as the mean or mid-point between two poles, one of which is an excess of the quality and the other a corresponding deficiency. This, strictly speaking, is not an acceptable form of the reconciliation of opposites, since the mean position is not a co-existence of the two poles, but rather a diminution of certain qualities in both. The most frequent form of 'extremes meet' in Coleridge is the simple paradox, by which when A and B are at polar extremes they partake of the same qualities, without any synthesis or 'higher third' to link them. Socrates gives an example of this in the *Philebus*, when he points out that extremes of pleasure and pain can lead to the same sensation.[36] Hegel was fascinated by the phenomenon and gave countless examples—'summa jus,

* See Appendix C.

summa injuria'; history shows that extreme anarchy veers into despotism; pride comes before a fall; too much wit outwits itself; 'the deepest melancholy will at times betray its presence by a smile'.[37]

This was exactly the sort of oddity that Coleridge found irresistibly intriguing. Can nothingness have a shape?—Yes, shadow. 'The thing that causes instability in another state—of itself causes stability—as for instance wet soap slips off the ledge, detain it till it dries a little and it *sticks*.'[38] A net to catch fish both catches them and lets a few slip through the meshes for the preservation of the species—'so two races are saved, the one by taking part, the other by part not being taken'.[39] An Iceland geyser can scald you with its spray, so an icy woman (like Mrs Coleridge) can have paroxysms of boiling rage.[40] There was nothing more satisfying than a paradox. It was nature's way of revealing the universal law. So Mr Flosky in *Nightmare Abbey* expressed his views on modern literature:

Modern literature is a north-east wind—a blight of the human soul. I take credit to myself for having helped to make it so. The way to produce fine fruit is to blight the flower. You call this a paradox. Marry, so be it. Ponder thereon.[41]

The fourth, and final, problem is this: What were the philosophical and theological implications of this form of thinking, eccentric and dated although so much of it may seem? What it amounts to is that truth *is* 'Yes *and* No, but neither'. The function of a synthesis is not to eradicate the separate identities of thesis and antithesis which must co-exist. This is not an unfamiliar concept to theologians. Indeed *coincidentia oppositorum* is deeply imbedded in Protestant theology, most particularly in Luther's doctrine of grace, the inner secret of which is the realization that the justified sinner is *simul justus et peccator*.[42] Modern theologians have come more and more to see theology as a process of dialectic, but have not always realized that Coleridge expressed every theological proposition in that form. Karl Barth, for instance, has written in *The Word of God and the Word of Man* that: 'if you ask about God, and if I am really to tell about him, dialectic is all that can be expected from me. . . . And therefore I have never affirmed

53

without denying, and never denied without affirming, for neither affirmation nor denial can be final.' And again: 'The truth lies not in the Yes and in the No but in the knowledge of the beginning from which the Yes and the No arise.'[43]

Coleridge would have approved of that; and so would F. D. Maurice. They saw that if truth lies at *both* the poles, the cardinal error of man is to suppose that a single pole can contain the whole of the truth. Maurice in his *Moral and Metaphysical Philosophy* vehemently defended Plato against the charge of eclecticism. His genius lay not in accommodation, but in *distinction*.[44] Truth is not a muddled form of compromise. It is imperative to distinguish truth from falsehood; but truth is almost always wider than we suppose. The process of analysing the opinions of others is to discover where they go wrong; and usually the error lies in their over-statement of their own belief to the exclusion of the opposite belief of their adversary. Thereby they convert their own vision of truth into a half-truth. The quest for truth, therefore, involves the recognition not only that most men are testifying to it, but also that they are deluded by the temptation to over-state it.

This—to Maurice—was Plato's greatest genius;* and in defending Plato he was also defending himself. If Plato, through Socrates, often appeared to mock the Sophists, at least he paid them the compliment of taking their teaching seriously; and if Socrates sometimes won his contests with them by unfair means, at least—when confronted with the greater metaphysical questions—he allowed both sides to have their say, and having submitted both viewpoints to logical examination left the reader to form his own conclusion.

Coleridge understood Plato in exactly the same way. His works, he said, 'are preparatory exercises for the mind. He leads you to see, that propositions involving in themselves contradictory conceptions, are nevertheless true; and which, therefore, must belong to a higher logic—that of ideas. They are contradictory only in the Aristotelian logic, which is the instrument of the understanding.'[45] The most striking testimony to F. D. Maurice's standpoint, however, is the fact that those thinkers who have expressed a similar view—that the quest for

---

* For a further discussion of F. D. Maurice's Platonism, see Appendix D.

truth really involves a critical dialectic of half-truths—have all, both before and after him, been drawn towards the Platonic tradition: in England, such figures as Archbishop Leighton, Coleridge, Julius Hare, F. W. Robertson and Brooke Foss Westcott; on the Continent, most prominent of all—Leibniz.

Coleridge almost certainly derived this idea himself from Leibniz and transmitted it to the English thinkers who came after him. It was Leibniz's dictum that one should 'never be too ready to despise or to condemn'.[46] Whereas Hegel—according to Walter Kaufmann—believed that men were usually wrong in their affirmations and right in their negations,[47] Leibniz had taught the very opposite. Men are usually right in what they affirm, and wrong in what they deny. Time and time again, Coleridge would testify to the truth of this.[48] Every work must be judged by its beauties rather than by its defects.[49] It is better to believe too much than too little.[50] Never dismiss a doctrine lightly.[51] Avoid violent criticism—for scholars sometimes delude themselves into thinking that they enhance their own stature by attacking the errors of others, when in reality they are merely indulging in the 'abominable vice of vulgar minds'. 'The moment you perceive the slightest spirit of envy in a man, be assured he either has no genius or that his genius is dormant at that moment; for all genius exists in a participation of a common spirit.'[52] There was a world of difference between a strong mind (such as Burke's) and a great mind (such as Swedenborg's). 'A great mind must be androgynous. Great minds . . . are never wrong.'[53]

Listen, then, to Coleridge's last testimony to this undying truth, recorded in the *Table-Talk*, the year being 1831:

My system, if I may venture to give it so fine a name, is the only attempt I know ever made to reduce all knowledge into harmony. It opposes no other system, but shows what was true in each; and how that which was true in the particular in each of them became error, *because* it was only half the truth. I have endeavoured to unite the insulated fragments of truth, and therewith to frame a perfect mirror. I show to each system that I fully and rightfully appreciate what that system means; but then I lift up that system to a higher point of view, from which I enable it to see its former position, where it was, indeed, but under another light and with different relations;—so that the fragment of truth is not only acknowledged, but explained.[54]

From Coleridge to Julius Hare; from Hare[55] to Maurice; from Maurice and the Mauriceans to the present day. It is the richest ingredient of Coleridge's thought, and acknowledged as such by John Stuart Mill. As is well known, Mill applied the Coleridgean formula in his own estimate of the dual influence of Coleridge and Bentham on nineteenth-century thought. They were the two 'opposite poles of one great force of progression'.[56] If the genius of the one could be united with that of the other, if extremes could meet in that sense, then their two seemingly opposite affirmations would form the corpus of truth. Bentham could never have been made to see the force of that. Coleridge, by the logic of his own arguments, would have been obliged to concede it. And yet, Mill observed, such a synthesis would be in some way less satisfactory than the continuing existence of the two poles which created a tension between them and a genuine dialectic.

Perhaps, then, great minds (which to Coleridge were androgynous) have to belong, by Mill's definition, to 'one-eyed men'. He argues thus:

There is hardly anything positive in Bentham's philosophy which is not true. . . . The bad part of his writings is his resolute denial of all that he does not see, of all truths but those which he recognises. . . . To reject his half of the truth because he overlooked the other half, would be to fall into his error without having his excuse. For our own part, we have a large tolerance for one-eyed men, provided their one eye is a penetrating one: if they see more, they would probably not see so keenly, nor so eagerly pursue one course of inquiry. Almost all rich veins of original and striking speculation have been opened by systematic half-thinkers.[57]

There is a note of realism on which to end. But it does not weaken (nor was it intended to) Coleridge's—and Plato's—perception of the nature of truth.

4

Coleridge and Newman

When F. D. Maurice drew a comparison between the Platonism of Cambridge and the Aristotelianism of Oxford, he had in mind two particular figures. The one was Coleridge, not so much because he was Cambridge-educated but because of the influence of Coleridge's teaching on certain prominent Cambridge figures; the other was Newman, whom he described as 'an eminent Aristotelian divine',[1] and whose reputation at Oxford in the year 1836 was just about at its height. To somebody with Maurice's particular philosophical and theological interests, it was an obvious and natural comparison to draw.

Coleridge and Newman differed in many significant respects; so much so, Newman himself said, that although he could learn from Coleridge he could never follow him. He conceded that Coleridge was 'a very original thinker, who, while he indulged a liberty of speculation which no Christian can tolerate, and advocated conclusions which were often heathen rather than Christian, yet after all instilled a higher philosophy into inquiring minds, than they had hitherto been accustomed to accept. In this way he made trial of his age, and found it respond to him, and succeeded in interesting its genius in the cause of Catholic truth.'[2] Setting aside the somewhat gratuitous tone of this, we may say that Newman's criticism amounted to an acknowledgement that Coleridge had rightly rejected the paltry Lockean philosophy of the eighteenth century and had discovered a surer way to truth; but unfortunately his over-speculative mind had bedimmed his vision so that he did not arrive at the truth in the end. Certainly he did not arrive at Newman's own position; and it may be worth while for a moment to consider whether some of the more important differences between them accounted for that fact.

Mr J. D. Boulger has argued that 'the divergence between Coleridge and Newman is essentially that between Protestant and Catholic thinking'.[3] This does not mean that their intellectual strivings followed a parallel course until Coleridge reached a *ne plus ultra* which for Newman did not exist, so that Newman arrived at a logical terminus which was temperamentally inaccessible to Coleridge. While both men were working out an epistemology in the course of a personal spiritual odyssey—Coleridge in his transition from Unitarianism to Anglican Trinitarianism and Newman in his passage from Calvinist Evangelicalism to Roman Catholicism—they were nevertheless wrestling with entirely different spiritual problems. It is true that at one stage both men were in the position of working out some form of reconciliation theory. Coleridge attempted to apply his law of polarity to the doctrines of the Christian faith in order to find a *rationale* for the doctrine of the Trinity which he had not understood before. Newman advanced a reconciliation theory as a *rationale* for the Anglican Church, presenting it as the *via media* between the corruption of Rome and the fanatical subjectivism of popular Protestantism.[4] And it is here that the fundamental difference shows itself.

In the first place, Coleridge's trichotomous logic was a variation on an essentially Platonic theme. Newman's *via media* was not. It was an attempt to work out an idea of the Christian Church on the basis of the Aristotelian mean; to present two opposites, the one a defect and the other an excess, and to find perfection in the virtue that lay between them.[5] Secondly, Coleridge was concerned with coming to terms with dogma, about which any form of philosophizing must amount, in Newman's terms of reference, to 'speculation'. Coleridge, with his particular conviction of the nature of reason to apprehend spiritual mysteries, would not have understood this charge. Newman, on the other hand, never had the slightest problem over dogma. From the age of fifteen, he tells us in the *Apologia*, 'dogma has been the fundamental principle of my religion; I know no other religion. . . . What I held in 1816, I held in 1833, and I hold in 1864. Please God, I shall hold it to the end.'[6]

Newman's problem was an institutional one. Where and what was the true Church? To put the matter at its simplest, this means that one has to discover by historical study what the true Church was. When you know this, you know what the Church should be like. 'Look on this picture and on that.'[7] By this process, the Aristotelian 'mean'—the *via media*—was found to be a logical monstrosity. It is interesting to see that by 1838, in the *Lectures on Justification*, Newman was already perceiving that logic forbids a middle position. Comparing the teaching of the Homilies on justifying faith with that of the Catholic Church, Newman realized that here were the two poles:

The one views it in the abstract, the other as it is in fact; the one considers it as the faith of the regenerate; the other as regenerate faith. *Either* notion is intelligible, whichever is the more advisable; but what is not at all intelligible is the notion of the Protestant schools, which makes it neither of one nor the other, but more than one and less than the other, something between abstract and concrete.[8]

Those who shy away from the extremes are those 'who pitch their tent in the very middle of their route, dread to go forward, and burn at the notion of going back'.[9] This is to say, abandoning the *via media* means a confrontation with an 'Either-Or'; it could never be Coleridge's way of 'Both-And'.

Mr Boulger argues that this is a Catholic mind at work. It betrays a fear of the subjective, distrust of the intuitive and a recourse to a scholastic form of thinking.[10] Newman certainly despised any attitude of mind that tended to put trust in man rather than in God, for this was the very essence of rationalism which led, among Christians, to Socinianism.[11] He believed that this was precisely Coleridge's temptation. Graham Hough has expressed the contrast well: 'Coleridge's concern to found doctrine on the intuition of Reason rather than on the *ipse dixit* of Revelation appears mere philosophical shadow-boxing. . . . To take an analogy from the moral sphere, it is the difference between a man who says "it is wrong because it is forbidden" and the man who says "it is forbidden because it is wrong".'[12] The role of reason with regard to revelation, according to Newman, was to make logical inferences from what was *given*. This was not all that was necessary, because reason is not the whole of man; and in making the greatest decisions of his life (such as a decision involving his salvation) 'the whole man moves'.[13] But granted that the mind is prepared to consider as an initial premise 'that there is a living God', then the divine revelation may be expected to evoke a response from that principle of right spiritual judgment in man which Newman described as 'the *organum investigandi* given us for gaining religious truth, and which would lead the mind by an infallible succession from the rejection of atheism to theism, and from theism to Christianity, and from Christianity to Evangelical Religion, and from these to Catholicity'.[14] Newman's was, indeed, a very Catholic mind.

Both Coleridge and Newman were Romantics, but they wore their romanticism with a difference. Newman, for instance, had little respect for the claims of the poetic imagination, as expressed by Wordsworth and Coleridge, and he was profoundly distrustful of their concept of symbolism. Christianity is more than a set of symbolical truths, conveyed in a mystical language, or the means of grace preserved by certain sacramental acts. Both the symbols and the sacraments are rooted in history; they are facts and events as well as signs. Coleridge was not blind to this, but it has to be admitted that his own historical sense was far less keen than Newman's. He had little feeling for history, and his passion for a somewhat indiscriminate plundering of ancient wisdom, in the spirit—one sometimes feels—of the least credible the better, worked against refined historical judgment. Indeed, he admitted the insensitivity himself:

Dear Walter Scott and myself [he once said] were exact, but harmonious, opposites in this;—that every old ruin, hill, river or tree called up in his mind a host of historical or biographical associations, ... whereas for myself, notwithstanding Dr Johnson, I believe I should walk over the plain of Marathon without taking more interest in it than any other plain of similar features.[15]

Coleridge's insensitivity to context may have been his chief weakness as a philosopher. For him, ideas were interesting only in so far as they could help him in his own quest for a universal law. He delved into the past to find out what people had said

rather than why they had said it. Newman's problem, or
deficiency, was a different one. He was a Catholic first and an
historian afterwards. Professor Chadwick has pictured him
tormented by some internal conflict when, in the course of
writing the *Apologia*, he so frequently alluded to the subject of
doctrinal development. There is displayed 'a certain inco-
herence or self-contradiction, . . . which may be a sign partly
of Newman's longing to hold that which is orthodox, that
which the Church taught, and yet of his historical and critical
conviction that he must not disregard uncomfortable evidence'.[16] But he knew where his duty lay. He tried, without
success, to persuade Acton that an historical judgment must
give way to ecclesiastical authority if the two should be in conflict,[17] and he thought very little of Döllinger for his error in
making history 'the supreme arbiter of what we were to
believe'.[18] This was where Protestants repeatedly fell down.
'They seem to me to expect from History more than History
can furnish', he wrote. 'He who believes the dogmas of the
Church only because he has reasoned them out in History, is
scarcely a Catholic.'[19]

Now if it were true to say that an historian is by nature more
inclined to be an Aristotelian than a Platonist, this comparison
between Coleridge and Newman might help us to elucidate
the central problem. Unfortunately no such facile statement
can be made. R. G. Collingwood, as is well known, believed
that historical enquiry was a process of Platonic dialectic—
'the dialogue of the soul with itself'.[20] Coleridge, in a discussion
recorded in the *Table Talk*, would appear to have regarded the
historian's method as essentially one of Aristotelian induction.
'The author professes to find out the truth by collecting the
facts of the case, and tracing them downwards.' This, he said,
was inferior to the philosophical approach, described as follows: 'You must . . . commence with the philosophic idea of
the thing, the true nature of which you wish to find out and
manifest. You must carry your rule ready made, if you wish
to measure aright.'[21]

This surely is a most illuminating remark for an understanding of both Coleridge and Newman. Both followed exactly the
same process here in their handling of institutions. In the first

place, they assessed the nature of any institution by reference to some original idea of it; secondly, although they conceived of institutions as organic and subject to development, neither of them applied the Aristotelian or teleological approach. John Stuart Mill observed this facet in Coleridge's study of the Church of England, and welcomed it. Whereas a Benthamite would pose the question—'what good does this institution serve and to what end is it moving?'—Coleridge's approach was conservative. He determined the nature of the Church of England from what its original purpose had been.[22] This, indeed, is the real distinction between the Benthamite question 'is it true?' and the Coleridgean approach, 'what is the meaning of it?'[23]

Here, too, Newman is on Coleridge's side. The principle of development within the Church is determined by its beginning not by the end to which it is moving.[24] The idea of a University, similarly, is discovered not in what it might become but in what it has been.[25] And what of Christianity itself—the living idea which has changed the world? In one of the most celebrated passages that Newman ever wrote, from the *Essay on Development*, he gave the answer. The last words—the most often quoted—might seem to represent the quintessence of organic Aristotelianism, but the context proves them to be not so. An idea, Newman writes, as time goes on 'enters upon strange territory. . . . Old principles reappear under new forms. It changes with them in order to remain the same. In a higher world it is otherwise, but here below to live is to change, and to be perfect is to have changed often.'[26]

This is much more an expression of Platonism than of Aristotelianism. The One remains. In the higher world, an idea does not change. Change is the condition of the imperfect world here below, where it is a necessity for new forms to shape the old idea so that it can remain the same. Therefore the student of philosophy, of theology, or of institutional growth must tend to look back rather than forward. Everything must be judged in relation to the original idea.

Where, then, does Newman's Aristotelianism lie? Partly in his understanding of the harmony between logic and rhetoric; partly, also, in his epistemology. Newman had very little time for formal logic. Nevertheless there was a period in his life, as a young Fellow of Oriel, when he was directly under the influence of Richard Whately, whose avowed intent with regard to his pupils was to engender in them a lasting respect for the spirit and method of Aristotelian logic. Newman had already encountered Aristotle's *Ethics* and the *Rhetoric* in his undergraduate years. Under Whately, his study concentrated, via Aldrich's *Rudiments of Logic*, on logic and rhetoric. He was closely associated with Whatley's work on both these subjects for the *Encyclopaedia Metropolitana*, and was permitted by Whately to transcribe a number of his papers and dialogues for his own private use.[27]

What this rigorous, and perhaps somewhat stylized, training in the disputatious arts meant to Oxford men in general is not very easy to describe. In Newman's years as an undergraduate at Trinity the training for Oxford 'Greats' had not been systematized in the way in which it was to become, with an overwhelming emphasis on logic, ethics and Bishop Butler's *Sermons in the Rolls Chapel*; but in working so closely with Whately, Newman had some hand in the shaping of the system. Two things, however, are clear. Firstly, the logic taught was meant to be applied. As Professor Dwight Culler has put it: 'in substance (Whately) added little or nothing to Aldrich, but in spirit he prepared the way for Mill. He brought logic out of Latin and into English, out of the disputation into the daily converse of men, out of the memory and into the understanding—but it remained the same logic as before.'[28]

Secondly, it tended to engender an attitude of mind; or at least a fastidiousness in exposition and in setting out the limit of one's enquiry, which gave to an Oxford man who had absorbed his reading seriously an unmistakable mintmark, a striving for definition or settling the meaning of one's words, combined with a sensitivity for every conceivable qualification.

In Gladstone this could become the language of a schoolman. When asked where the Peelites should sit in the House of Commons, his reply was: 'Taking a seat is an external sign and pledge that ought to follow upon full conviction of the thing it is understood to betoken.'[29] This was the reply of an Oxford man with a First in Greats. There is an exactitude about it, and an undoubted pedantry, which belongs to an entirely different world from the opaque language of Coleridge and F. D. Maurice, for all the anxiety of the former to give to individual words ultra-precise meanings. A particularly fine parody of the Oxford Aristotelian manner occurs in *Loss and Gain*, when Charles Reding is conversing with his family and Mr Malcolm on the power of scent as opposed to the power of sound:

'Well, sir, but think of this', said Charles: 'scents are complete in themselves, yet do not consist of parts. Think how very distinct the smell of a rose is from a pink, a pink from a sweet-pea, a sweet-pea from a stock, a stock from lilac. . . . And these are only the scents of flowers; how different flowers smell from fruits, fruits from spices, spices from roast beef or pork cutlets, and so on. Now, what I was coming to is this—these scents are perfectly distinct from each other, and *sui generis*; they never can be confused; yet each is communicated to the apprehension in an instant. Sights take up a great space, a tune is a succession of sounds: but scents are at once specific and complete, yet indivisible. Who can halve a scent? They need neither time nor space; thus they are immaterial or spiritual.'

'Charles hasn't been to Oxford for nothing', said his mother, laughing and looking at Mary; 'this is what I call chopping logic.'[30]

This is unmistakably Newman—the charm, the subtlety, the love of distinction, the diction. And everything that Newman wrote bore this mintmark. Compare, for instance, Coleridge's tortured convolutions in making epistemological definitions—sometimes emerging with a lucid sentence, but when it comes it is the solitary rose amongst a patch of briar—with the severely exact opening chapter of the *Grammar of Assent*, or the syllogistic form of the argument of the first two discourses of the *Idea of a University*.[31] Better still, compare for their similarity Charles Reding's logic-chopping with the superb passage in the *Idea*, where Newman himself writes of sights and sounds as sensed by men and brutes. The intellect of man, he tells us—

seizes and unites what the senses present to it; it grasps and forms what need not have been seen or heard except in its constituent parts. It discerns in lines and colours, or in tones, what is beautiful and what is not. It gives them a meaning, and invests them with an idea. . . . It distinguishes between rule and exception, between accident and design. It assigns phenomena to a general law, qualities to a subject, acts to a principle, and effects to a cause. In a word, it philosophizes.[32]

Note, too, the exactitude and subtlety of the closing sentence of this section: 'We cannot do without a view, and we put up with an illusion, when we cannot get a truth.'[33]

This is a long way from Aristotle, no doubt—but have logic and rhetoric ever been so consummately combined? Whately provided Newman's hyper-sensitive mind with a framework, a set of tools, or—more appositely—an armoury of weapons, which he could adapt with devastating effect for polemical use. He could criticize Aristotle, and did so in a penetrating essay on the inadequacy of Aristotle's *Poetics*,[34] but—as Whately must have ruefully observed in later life—to be criticized by Newman was a sure acknowledgment of an earlier discipleship. Although Newman discarded Whately, he never forgot what Whately had taught him. In method and style he remained an Aristotelian for the rest of his life.

This is well seen in two of his greatest works—*The Idea of a University* and *The Grammar of Assent*. In the *Idea*, Newman referred to Aristotle as often as not by the appellation accorded to him by St Thomas and Dante 'the Great Philosopher'. And, in Discourse V, when he is extolling the inductive method, he pays Aristotle his finest tribute:

While the world lasts, will Aristotle's doctrine on these matters last, for he is the oracle of nature and of truth. While we are men, we cannot help, to a great extent, being Aristotelians, for the great Master does but analyse the thoughts, feelings, views, and opinions of human kind. He has told us the meaning of our words and ideas, before we were born. In many subject-matters, to think correctly is to think like Aristotle: and we are his disciples, whether we will or no though we may not know it.[35]

It was precisely the intimate relationship between logic and rhetoric, between thought and expression, which Newman was so anxious to impart. 'Style is the man.' This we learn from Aristotle's celebrated sketch of the magnanimous man, whose 'style is not only the image of his subject, but of his mind'; it follows that 'the elocution of a great intellect is great'.[36] The matter is taken further in the discourse on 'University Preaching'. While rhetoric is there truly presented as the art of knowing one's audience, persuasion does not proceed from display but from character. As Aristotle taught, the most cogent argument is the ethical nature of the man who is presenting it, and accordingly 'the common sense of the world decides that it is safer, where it is possible, to commit oneself to the judgment of men of character than to any consideration addressed merely to the feelings or to the reason'.[37] A rationalist, like Paley, may prove; but it is man, a human being, who persuades. And because he is what he is, he appeals not only to reason but to the whole man. In an earlier essay on 'Prospects of the Anglican Church', Newman pointed to the importance of finding the right medium or calculus of exposition:

A problem which continually meets us is, how to express the truth of one province of knowledge in the terms of another. . . . What is the art of rhetoric but the reduction of reasonings, in themselves sound, into the calculus of the tastes, opinions, passions and aims of a particular audience?[38]

So we have the link with the very Aristotelian argument of the *Grammar of Assent*. Two crucial aspects of Newman's epistemology, as worked out in the *Grammar*, may be mentioned here—the first, the role of mental antecedents; the second, the nature and range of the illative sense. In the first place, Newman argues that all reasoning must be able to stand up to the accepted logical tests, in the form of syllogisms, propositions, logical inferences and the like. But while logic may be unimpeachable, the fact remains that one man may be convinced by it, even if weakly presented, and another man may find it utterly unacceptable even if the argument cannot at any point be challenged. Men accept or refute evidence according to the state of their hearts.[39]

What, then, is this 'state of heart' or character of mind which determines one's deepest decisions? It is, firstly, that set of antecedent assumptions which predispose this person or that to certain first principles as opposed to others. A certain type of theist, however strong his arguments, will make no sort of impression upon a convinced atheist.[40] As Aristotle himself taught, a mathematical mind will be convinced by abstractions while the practical mind will demand an empirical approach, the experience of facts.[41] So there is in man some instinctive or intuitive reason which operates particularly within the field in which this or that person can acquire a particular skill.

The general term to describe this faculty is the illative sense. It includes those 'elementary convictions of the mind' (as James Mozley defined antecedent assumptions),[42] and yet is wider than this, embracing the whole disposition, temper and 'fundamental modes of looking at things, which exist in the mind of the reasoner'.[43] It is, in fact, what Aristotle described as *phronesis* in the sphere of ethics, translated into the sphere of epistemology. *Phronesis* is the quality which enables us to make right judgments in matters of conduct; it is not an absolute truth, because one man's duty may differ from another's. Similarly, there must be in man a corresponding faculty—an *organum investigandi*—which enables him to come to a right judgment in matters of knowledge or truth as opposed to conduct.[44] And this, too, will be a very personal quality—the historical intuition of a mind like Niebuhr's, or a way of interpreting nature in a mind like Bishop Butler's.[45] But it goes beyond mental antecedents, since it operates beyond the determination of first principles, the measure of its range being 'the start, the course, and the issue of an inquiry'.[46]

This definition of the illative sense was the climax of Newman's epistemological enquiries, looking back to his first university sermon on the relationship between character and right belief,[47] to the incomparable distinction between the power of dogma and the puny uninvolvement of purely intellectual assent as expressed in his essay on the Tamworth Reading Room, and finding its final expression in Newman's chosen cardinalatial motto, which summarized the labour of a lifetime in defining the limits of logic and rational enquiry—*cor ad cor loquitur*, heart speaks to heart. *How* the heart appeals to the heart of another is the deepest secret of rhetoric; how the heart responds to the appeal of another lies in the working of the illative sense. And on both these questions Newman found the answer in Aristotle. 'Such is Aristotle's doctrine', he wrote in the *Grammar of Assent* on the concept of *phronesis,* 'and it is undoubtedly true.'[48]

But we have heard all this before; or, at least, something very like it. What is this heart speaking to heart but the very essence of Romanticism, that interconnection of thought and feeling, knowledge and divination, expressed by those in England and in Germany who were finding in Plato a theory of intuitive perception which emancipated them from philosophies of sensationalism, belonging to the tradition of Aristotle and Locke? And, returning to the original comparison, we may ask how does this differ from Coleridge, whose epistemological enquiries all led up to one 'inimitable truth' as he expressed it in *The Friend:*

WHAT COMES FROM THE HEART, THAT ALONE GOES TO THE HEART; WHAT PROCEEDS FROM A DIVINE IMPULSE, THAT THE GODLIKE ALONE CAN AWAKEN.[49]

The answer is that there was very little difference, except that the truth had been arrived at by a different route. Indeed, the conclusions that Coleridge and Newman shared are far more striking than their differences. Coleridge tells us that a child has a vision of the vast and a poetic grasp of unity which a philosopher may only with a struggle regain. Newman pictures an infant stretching out its arms to grasp its 'many-coloured vision', which time and experience will cut up into parts. But 'the first view was the more splendid, the second the more real; the former more poetical, the latter more philosophical. Alas! what are we doing all through life . . . but unlearning the world's poetry, and attaining to its prose!'[50]

How can we be sure of salvation? Newman asked himself as a young man; and answered 'I know I know. How? I know I know I know etc. etc.'[51] How do I know that my philosophical concept of reality is valid? asks Coleridge in the *Table Talk.* 'I answer, in the same way exactly that you know that your eyes were made to see with; and that is, because you *do* see with them.'[52] Our reception to this argument or that, says Newman, is always conditioned by antecedent premisses. Yes, suggests Coleridge before him, at the beginning there is a first principle. 'I assume a something, the proof of which no man can give to another, yet every man may find for himself. If any man assert that he cannot find it, I am bound to disbelieve him. I cannot do otherwise without unsettling the foundations of my own moral nature.'[53]

The similarities could be carried further. Just as a decision is more than intellectual acquiescence but rather the conviction of the whole man, so knowledge is itself a unity, an integration of the sciences ministering to the same truth and finding its highest point in philosophy and theology. In this sense, Newman's *Idea of a University*, one of the last great expositions of the assurance that knowledge is a circle and that the quest for it is vitiated by undue specialization, was anticipated in Coleridge's idea of an Encyclopaedia. 'To call a huge unconnected miscellany of the *omne scibile*, in an arrangement determined by the accident of initial letters, an encyclopaedia is the impudent ignorance of your Presbyterian book-makers', Coleridge exploded to Southey.[54] More positively, as he put it in the *Philosophical Lectures*, it should be 'a co-organisation of the sciences, as so many interdependent systems, each having a specific life of its own but all communicating with philosophy as the common centre or brain'.[55] Even in the word 'idea' itself, they were at one. As Dorothy Emmett has put it, in writing of Coleridge, an 'idea' is not just a definition; it embraces the 'attempt to describe the inner ethos or quality of something'.[56] This was exactly how Newman saw it, whether he were describing the idea of a university or that of the true Church.

It is clear that Newman was no metaphysician. The tone of his epistemological writings was totally different from Coleridge's, for he was concerned primarily with the ethical and practical implications of belief and certitude, and it is significant that he arrived at a theory of intuitive perception (the illative sense) through the Aristotelian concept of *phronesis* rather than from Platonic metaphysical teaching on innate ideas. It was for this reason that Dean Inge came to the conclusion that 'no more misleading statement could be made about Newman's philosophy than to associate him with Platonism of any kind, whether Pagan or Christian'.[57]

I cannot accept this. Although Newman was brought up on

the Aristotelian tradition, he came through his friendship with Keble, Pusey and Froude to concentrate his studies, during the late 1820's and 1830's, on the early Church fathers, notably Clement, Origen and Dionysius—the Alexandrian Platonists. In these he encountered metaphysics in abundance, the theory of universals and the teaching on the unsubstantial nature of the material world. Such teaching could not fail to impress him. It was different; it threw fresh light on the nature of man and his destiny. Also it struck a chord in his memory. As a boy he had felt 'life to be a dream, or I an Angel, and all this world a deception'.[58] Here were the Alexandrian Platonists saying the same thing, confirming—as Athanasius had put it— the 'obviously symbolical character of all visible forms'.[59]

This did not convert Newman into a metaphysician, nor did it greatly affect his own epistemological thinking, although his use of Neoplatonic language in his *History of the Arians* gave rise to some doubts in the minds of his readers.[60] But something of this teaching adhered. In the *Stromatum* of Clement and the *De Principiis* of Origen, Newman encountered the doctrine of *oeconomia*. Indeed, the teaching on economy and the unsubstantiality of the material world were closely linked. 'What are the phenomena of the external world', wrote Newman in the *Arians*, 'but a divine mode of conveying to the mind the reality of existence, individuality, and the influence of being on being?'[61] It is true that he goes on to say that he cannot tell whether such a philosophy be true or false. But here is the Neoplatonic language of Newman's fellow-Romantics, who saw in the finite world glimpses of infinity, through their power to read the symbolism or to exercise the poetic imagination. Newman could not accept the Wordsworthian concept of nature;[62] but he could and did take hold of the doctrine of economy as the divine mode of revealing sacred truth. And with that he stepped at once into the world of the Neoplatonists, and found himself—perhaps without knowing it—translating into theological language the esoteric teaching of dedicated Platonists like Thomas Taylor and William Blake.

To Taylor and to Blake, the sublime teaching of the ancients, and Plato more than any, was shrouded in mystery. Their symbolism was intentionally obscure; their language deliberately opaque. And this for the very good reason that the deepest truths, beyond the comprehension of the ignorant multitude, should be hidden so that only those who were fit to appreciate the mysteries should receive them. The truth was like the sun's rays which would blind the prisoners in the cave were they to turn round from their absurd contemplation of the realm of shadows. Those whose eyes were strong enough to see the truth would do no service to the ignorant by teaching it in all its fullness. Sacred truths were a form of gnosis, only to be received by the initiated. In transmitting these truths, recourse must be made to symbols and enigmas, or—as G. M. Harper has put it—the cult of 'deliberate obscurity'.[63]

This was how Thomas Taylor presented Plato and the Neoplatonists to his disciples; and this is exactly how Blake responded. His poetry and pictures strive for the arcane and symbolical, even to the extent of deceptively simple language and a naïve metre or form in some of his poems, so that the unknowing can read them at their face-value without realizing that a deeper mystery is being uttered. As he said himself to Dr Trusler in 1799:

You ought to know that which is Grand is necessarily obscure to Weak men. That which can be made Explicit to the Idiot is not worth my care. The wisest of the Ancients considered what is not too Explicit as the fittest for Instruction, because it rouzes the faculties to act. I name Moses, Solomon, Esop, Homer, Plato.[64]

This is different from Coleridge's élitism as embodied in his teaching on the Clerisy, which also has good Platonic roots. But it is precisely the notion that 'pearls are not cast before swine', as understood by Newman from Keble's teaching on Reserve in communicating religious knowledge, and from the Alexandrian Platonists on the *disciplina arcani*—the underlying philosophy, in fact, of the religiosity and ecclesiology of the Oxford Movement.

So was Newman a Platonist or an Aristotelian? If Coleridge's famous aphorism is correct, we cannot escape by saying that he was a bit of both. The theology partook of a Platonic temper; there was an affinity between what Newman found in the Alexandrian Platonists and what he knew and felt from his

earliest experiences. His epistemology, however, was primarily
Aristotelian. So were his training, his method, his own estimate
of what he had learned from Oxford, where his soul ever remained. It takes an Oxford man to tell us what this means:

Often when I am reading Newman [G. M. Young has written], an
unholy analogy presents itself, and, as he would have said, 'stains my
imagination'. I cannot help thinking of those African virgins who in
Gibbon's language, 'admitted priests and deacons to their bed, and
gloried amidst the flames in their unsullied purity'. He is always
skimming along the verge of a logical catastrophe, and always rely-
ing on his dialectic agility to save himself from falling; always exposing what seems to be an unguarded spot, and always revealing a
new line of defence when the unwary assailant has reached it. I am
not sure it is not a general characteristic of Oxford: we are not the
children of Ockham for nothing: and we are all, I think, more ready
to take intellectual risks than they are at 'the less ancient and splendid'
place, trusting to Aristotle to inspire us with the right mood and
figure when needed, and so to preserve the 'unsullied purity' of our
reasoning.[65]

Oxford has a subtle power over her children; one cannot
doubt it. But in this instance, Newman answered our original
question in a way which no Oxford man would care to accept.
As a child he saw the vision whole, only to learn as he grew up
how it could be divided into parts. He unlearned the world's
poetry only to attain to its prose. And Maurice, then, was
right to correct Edward Strachey, who quoted Coleridge's
aphorism at him; right on Newman, at least. For here was a
child, if ever there was one, who was born a Platonist; and
how else did he become an Aristotelian but through his
education?

5

Plato and Incarnationalism

Three final questions should now be posed. How valid is the
claim that nineteenth-century Oxford was primarily Aristotelian in its teaching? In what sense can there be said to have
been a rival Platonic tradition at Cambridge? And, finally,
how can one explain the common emphasis on incarnationalism, with avowedly Platonic roots, in both Oxford and
Cambridge theology by the end of the century?

An examination of the Greats course at Oxford certainly
gives substance to the view that Aristotle predominated. In
the formalized structure which the Honour School of *Literae
Humaniores* obtained in 1830, there was no compulsory reading
of Plato (although the *Phaedrus* was considered advisable), but
a detailed study of four of Aristotle's writings was required—
the *Nicomachean Ethics*, the *Politics*, the *Rhetoric* and the *Poetics*.[1]
Alongside Aristotle was the very Aristotelian Bishop Butler,
notably his *Analogy* and the *Sermons at the Rolls Chapel*, which
became compulsory reading for Greats in 1833. Matthew
Arnold, who was expressly sent to Oxford by his father to gain
the priceless Oxford training in Aristotelian rhetoric, compared
the reverent devotion accorded to Butler and Aristotle with
the way in which Scottish students were brought up on the
Bible. 'Your text-book was right; there were no mistakes *there*.
If there was anything obscure, anything hard to be comprehended, it was your ignorance which was in fault, your failure
of comprehension.'[2] Goldwin Smith described Butler's *Analogy*
as 'the Oxford Koran . . . a universal solvent of the theological
difficulties',[3] and Gladstone, in 1860, when times were changing
and the Greats course was coming under fire, ignored such

foolish, modish talk and gave to his son Herbert, just going into residence, some sound, traditional advice:

With respect to philosophy . . . I should recommend you as three books Aristotle's 'Ethics' and 'Politics' and Butler's 'Analogy'. You should also read and know Butler's sermons. . . . I cannot say what value I attach to Bishop Butler's works. Viewing him as a guide of life, especially for the intellectual difficulties and temptations of these times, I place him before any other author. The *spirit* of wisdom is in every line.[4]

In a later letter to Herbert, Gladstone explained the rival merits of the two philosophical systems:

The merit of Plato's philosophy is in a quasi-spiritual and highly imaginative element that runs through it; Aristotle's deals in a most sharp, searching and faithful analysis of the facts of human life and human nature. All the reasons that have bound Aristotle so wonderfully to Oxford should, I think, recommend him to you.[5]

The implication is that Plato is airy, fanciful and metaphysical; Aristotle, by comparison, more practical, more down-to-earth, more scientific. That this was less than just to Plato, many of his nineteenth-century devotees were at pains to demonstrate. No one doubted that Aristotle was a master of the inductive and empirical method, or that the *Ethics* and the *Politics* were supreme in establishing the validity of inferring general principles from the study of particulars. Plato, according to Aristotle himself, was not so easy to label. 'Plato rightly used to doubt and question', Aristotle wrote in the *Ethics*, 'whether the way was from principles or to principles, as, in the stadium, whether from the judges to the goal, or reversely.'[6] It is interesting, therefore, to find Coleridge, F. D. Maurice and John Stuart Mill all arguing strongly that Plato was as inductive a thinker as Aristotle. Coleridge, for instance, described the Socratic method as inductive because he taught that 'the only way to arrive at a just definition was by a fair induction of all the particulars which could not be gained but by looking at them without prejudice and with a mind weaned from its selfish passions'.[7]

F. D. Maurice agreed. He recognized that Plato had a profound respect for mathematics, which might suggest a tendency towards *a priori* reasoning. But the process of mathematical demonstration by way of 'axioms, definitions, hypotheses, propositions' held no attraction for Plato. It 'has scarcely a Socratic element in it'. The Socratic—Platonic quest was rather to study visible objects in order to find in them the permanent forms and principles which lay behind them. In this respect Plato's induction was superior to that of Aristotle, who did not share his suspicion of phenomena and took things far too much at their face value, thus becoming 'the parent of all the modern schools of sensible philosophy'.[8]

John Stuart Mill could not go the whole way with this interpretation of Plato's method. Plato was an inductive thinker, always *'dividing down* to the thing which is the subject of enquiry', but Aristotle created the science of induction by showing it to be 'the ultimate ground and wisdom of all our knowledge'.[9] Mill's purpose was to distinguish between the Plato of the Dialogues and the wild speculation which came after him, either Neoplatonism ('a hybrid product of Greek and Oriental speculation')[10] or Transcendentalism ('the German Ontology', a mass of 'vague abstractions', hidden 'under a superficial varnish of modern inductive philosophy').[11] He had no time for the metaphysical side of Greek thought. In ancient Greece, he wrote, 'wisdom was not something to be prattled about, but something to be done. It was this which, during the bright days of Greece, prevented them from degenerating into vain and idle refinements, and produced that rare combination which distinguishes the great minds of that glorious people— of profound speculation, and business-like matter-of-fact common sense.'[12]

There you have the nineteenth century speaking—or, at least, that part of it which was not carried away by the heady wine of the Neoplatonist Romantics. It expresses, too, the inner meaning and ultimate educational objective of Oxford Greats. The Greats course was designed to inculcate practical wisdom, moral thoughtfulness and the judiciousness and tact of the public man. In so far as *phronesis* could be taught, the Greats course tried to teach it. It is, perhaps, as Newman put it, attaining to the world's prose while losing its poetry; or—as Aristotle distinguishes it in the *Ethics*—a quality of seasoned prudence as opposed to intuitive intelligence.[13] It is what Gladstone meant when he praised above all else the spirit of wisdom in Bishop Butler. Walter Bagehot has described it thus:

Now of the poetic religion there is nothing in Butler. . . . A young poet, not a very wise one, once said 'he did not like the Bible, there was nothing about flowers in it'. He might have said so of Butler with great truth: a most ugly and stupid world one would fancy *his* books were written in. But in return and by way of compensation for this, there is a religion of another sort, a religion the source of which is within the mind as the other's was to be found in the world without; the religion . . . of *superstition*. The source of this, as most persons are practically aware, is in the conscience.[14]

In 1825 a new magazine was launched in Oxford, entitled the *Oxford Quarterly Magazine*. Its life was pitifully short, but its purposes were high, as proclaimed by its opening editorial which set out to explain to the world why the Oxford curriculum was second to none. The main glory was that it fitted 'her disciples for the world'. And the reason why was because her studies were rooted in Aristotle. From the *Rhetoric* was learnt 'METHOD . . . which distinguishes the scholar from the unlettered multitude'. But the pinnacle was reached with the *Ethics*, from which was derived 'an exercise for thought superior . . . to any production of the heathen world'. It was salutary for a young man to discover that there is nothing new under the sun. 'Many a maxim which, when advanced by some popular theorist of the day, had been extolled for its sagacity . . . might be traced to its source in the Nicomachean Ethics of Aristotle.'[15]

The Greats course was to change. In 1860 Bishop Butler's works came off the list of compulsory reading. Through the championship of William Sewell, and then of Mark Pattison and Jowett,[16] the Platonic dialogues began to creep in. In 1847 the first Plato question appeared in the Logic paper—on the concept of *anamnesis*, interestingly enough.[17] The *Republic* became a set text, largely through the influence of Jowett. 'Germs of all ideas are to be found in Plato', he would say. 'Aristotle is dead, but Plato is alive.'[18] His Platonism, however, owed nothing to the influence of Coleridge and Maurice; its roots were Germanic, and primarily Hegelian. Jowett's long acquaintance with the writings of Hegel, and his own massive work on the dialogues of Plato, enabled him to make a deep impression on the Oxford of the second half of the nineteenth century, quite apart from the personal sway which he exercised as Tutor and then Master of Balliol. It is seen most directly in R. L. Nettleship and perhaps more significantly in T. H. Green.

But Plato did not oust Aristotle from the Greats course. It would be more accurate to say that the course was widened to include him, along with certain modern philosophers, notably Bacon, Kant and Mill. In a volume published in 1878, purporting to give advice to freshmen, the editor—A. M. M. Stedman—described Oxford culture as an amalgam of Aristotle's *Ethics* and Plato's *Republic*. The *Ethics* was the vital text, however, to be read through 'at least four times, and more, if time can be found'.[19] In a later edition, published nine years later, the same editor ventured to sum up Oxford Moral Philosophy with the sentence: 'Know your Republic and Ethics, and you are safe.'[20] Mature reflection had, however, led him to recommend a tougher stint on Aristotle's *Ethics*. It should now be read through at least ten times, and very carefully at that.[21]

Oxford, like Sparta of old, absorbed a change by making it an accretion. Plato came alongside Aristotle, who was still the Master. Ernest Barker, who was an undergraduate in the days of Bradley, Cook Wilson and H. A. Prichard—all pupils or opponents of T. H. Green[22]—could still exclaim: 'what a fascination Aristotle had for many of the acutest minds in Oxford in those days'. At a tutorial with J. A. Smith, a copy of Aristotle's *De Anima* was looked for among his shelves and was not found. Smith 'hunted and hunted. . . . Finally he disappeared into his bedroom, and in a moment he returned in triumph. "I was reading it in bed last night," he explained, "and I had left it under my pillow." '[23] It was the most natural and spontaneous tribute to Oxford's presiding genius.

Throughout the century the underlying assumptions of the Greats course remained the same. It existed to produce the learned gentleman of humane letters, Aristotle's 'magnanimous man'. This was Newman's idea of a university, and it remained so to the end—'an *Alma Mater*, knowing her children one by one, not a foundry or a mint, or a treadmill';[24] founded on cultured talk, the collegiate environment, leisured study based on a common deposit of philosophical, classical and religious learning; in short—what many still suspect in their hearts— the perfect background and training for a career in public life or the liberal professions. In 1946, G. M. Young delivered the Foundation Oration at Birkbeck College in the University of London, and he indulged in a delightfully Oxonian fancy. 'If ever the Dark Ages return,' he said, 'and two books only come through, then, if those books are Aristotle's *Ethics* and Newman's *Idea of a University*, they will be enough to show a reviving world what civilization meant.'[25]

What equivalent two books could a Cambridge man offer? It would be convenient for the sake of the general thesis to represent Plato's *Republic* as one of them. This would not, however, be true. Cambridge never had the equivalent of the Oxford Greats course to stand as its peculiar cultural mint-mark. And when F. D. Maurice compared Oxford Aristotelianism to Cambridge Platonism, his chosen point of contrast was much more subtle than a straight setting in opposition of two different courses of study.

It must be remembered, first of all, that Maurice was speaking of the 1830's—a decade in which at Cambridge the stars of Coleridge and Wordsworth were in the ascendant. 'Coleridge and Wordsworth were our principal divinities', wrote Charles Merivale, 'and Hare and Thirlwall were regarded as their prophets.'[26] If there were divinities and prophets, there were the apostles too. The Cambridge Apostles, self-consciously as select a band as those who had achieved first classes in Oxford Greats, were (in R. C. Trench's words) 'a gallant band of Platonico-Wordsworthian-Coleridgean anti-Utilitarians'.[27] Coleridge could still be visited at Highgate; Wordsworth sometimes appeared in Cambridge itself. '*Virgilium vidi!*' reads a diary entry of John Allen, friend of Henry Alford. 'This day (20 November 1830) I saw William Wordsworth.'[28] 'Platonico-Wordsworthian' Coleridgeanism, as it was revered by F. D. Maurice, partook of two aspects. Negatively, it was anti-Benthamite; in a positive sense, it was an inter-

78

pretation of Christian doctrine (for that it must have been to Maurice who always thought and wrote as a theologian) which laid particular stress on the incarnation and its centrality within the Christian revelation. This must be briefly explained.

The word 'Logos' has a dual meaning within the context of revelation. It is the Creative Word, the Word of God from the beginning, and as such was used by Greek thinkers, notably Heraclitus, who employed it in the sense of universal reason permeating the whole world, and by the Stoics. Plato not only uses it as the archetypal idea—'the idea of ideas'—but equates it with the Creator or the divine energy in forming the world in the *Timaeus*, and pictures it as personified in his discussion in the *Republic* of good as the highest object of knowledge.[29] In the writings of Philo of Alexandria, the Johannine concept of *Logos* is most nearly reached by a syncretism of Platonic, Stoic and Hebraic elements, so that the Word is not only the divine reason immanent in the world, but the intermediary agent of God *within* the world and the act of creation itself. So Philo approached the hypostasis of the author of the fourth gospel, in which *Logos* assumes its second meaning—the Word becoming flesh, the Incarnation, the Second Person of the Trinity. As Westcott wrote, this was John's 'central affirmation', underlying all he wrote. 'He transferred to the region of history the phrases in which men before him had spoken of "the logos",—"the Word"—"the Reason"—in the region of metaphysics.'[30]

The early fathers, who were steeped in Platonism, could find in the interpretation of Philo an explanation for what appeared to be divine wisdom in Plato. The *Logos*, being none other than 'the universal and long-existing light of divine revelation' which was manifested in the fullness of its glory in Christ, was already operating in the world before the Word was made flesh. Not only the prophets and the patriarchs were uplifted and enlightened by the *Logos*, but also heathen philosophers. Plato wrote under divine guidance; and all such who were blessed with a vision of eternal truth must, according to Justin Martyr, be numbered among Christians and the blessed in heaven.[31] If this were accepted, the myths and allegories of Plato acquired a sort of arcane significance. They embraced divine truth communicated through the accommodating device of parables.[32] While Plato's moral teaching—the nature of love as expressed by Diotima in the *Symposium*, the superior insight which led him to repudiate the more primitive ethic of 'helping your friends and harming your enemies' and to teach instead that it is better to suffer than to do wrong—is the quintessence of Christian morality, the element which has most attracted theologians to him has been Plato's anticipation of the *Logos* doctrine as revealed in the fourth gospel. Platonists have tended, throughout history, to be incarnationalists; or, to express it more exactly, the disposition to place the Incarnation at the centre of one's theology (as opposed to the Redemption or the Atonement) has often been accompanied by a predilection for Plato as opposed to any other philosopher.

Throughout the history of the Christian Church one can discern something of a theological dialectic in process, the stress changing, like the swinging of a pendulum, from the centrality of 'Christus Redemptor' to the primacy of 'Christus Consummator', so that after a period when the Cross is represented as the supreme element in the relationship between God and man, there comes an attempt to redress the theological balance by emphasizing the *Logos* doctrine, the union of the Godhead with man, by the Word becoming flesh. This is hardly an instance of dialectical progression in the sense of thesis and antithesis because clearly the Incarnation and the Redemption are rather complementary aspects of the working of the divine grace than contrary manifestations of it. The two doctrines may be more properly represented as two sides of a single coin. They constitute a looking at the God–man relationship from two different points of view which can lead to profound differences of interpretation in the course of theological development.

The one, for instance, takes as its starting point the inherent sinfulness of man, the other the exaltation of humanity by the Word becoming flesh. The one is Pauline and Augustinian in its theological foundations; the other is Joannine. During the nineteenth century in England, the trend appears to have been towards an incarnational theology; and by the end of the century it had come to assume, in contradistinction to the particular incarnationalism of the Tractarians, a somewhat immanentist flavour. That is to say, it tended to emphasize the way in which man had been ennobled and elevated by the divine grace, so that man himself through his works and his writings could reveal God's purposes, because in some way the divine was reflected in him. It is not in the least surprising that such an interpretation of incarnational theology should at some stage find expression, since it so naturally falls into line— as Mr B. M. G. Reardon has recently pointed out—with a general tendency to conceive of development in evolutionary terms.[33] Hegel had expressed the concept of movement onwards through dialectical progression; Comte and Herbert Spencer, in their different ways, had looked to a future becoming ever brighter; and evolutionary theory had demonstrated that the collision of the brute forces of nature had resulted in a product (the human species) of limitless potential. The incarnationalists of the later nineteenth century were to translate evolutionary philosophy into theological terms.

Now where does Platonism fit in? Coleridge appears outrageously to simplify the theological dialectic by describing St Paul as an Aristotelian and St John as a Platonist. 'St Paul writes more particularly for the dialectic understanding', he tells us; 'and proves the doctrines which were capable of such proof by common logic. . . . It is delightful to think that the beloved Apostle was born a Plato. To him was left the most oracular utterance of the mysteries of the Christian religion.'[34] Dean Inge would rightly have nothing to do with such an absurd argument. One could hardly find a better exposition of pure Platonism than St Paul's 'the things that are seen are temporal, but the things that are not seen are eternal'. All Paulines are to some extent Platonists and the author of the fourth gospel was not in fact representing a different tradition.[35] It would be equally absurd to fail to discern the strong Platonic element in St Augustine, which Westcott seems to have done in eulogizing the essentially Greek theology of Origen as against a more formal and rigid Latin theology in St Augustine.[36]

Nevertheless Coleridge, at the beginning of the century, and Westcott, at the end, firmly believed that Plato had prepared the world for Christianity. As Coleridge put it, 'Plato had taught men that after going through all the highest exertions of the faculties which nature had given them, cultivating their senses, their understandings, their reason and their moral power, yet still there was a ground wanting, a something that could not be found within the sphere of their knowledge.'[37] Westcott's Christianity was a compound of Plato, St John and Origen, because in these three writers the nature of the *Logos* had been expressed in 'two great thoughts':

(1) that the whole world is a manifestation of the goodness and righteousness of GOD in every detail; and (2) that the moral determination of each individual is a decisive element in the working out of the Divine counsel. This compound conception of the sum of finite being as a unity, consistent with, or rather dependent upon, the free and responsible action of each individual, is evidently of the utmost significance. There can be none greater.[38]

It was this combination of perfect unity, on the one hand, with the recognition of the individuality of each finite being, on the other, perceived by Origen, which led Westcott to define Christianity as the 'Absolute Religion' in precisely the same terms. No other religion speaks, or has spoken, more perfectly to the needs of man. Christ came 'to effect the perfection no less than the redemption of finite being, . . . to bring a perfect unity of humanity without destroying the personality of any one man'.[39]

The Platonic allusions in Westcott's writings are so many that it would be impossible to enumerate them. Always, if he could, he would connect a Platonic reference with a Joannine development and the doctrine of the Incarnation. The myths of Plato were not 'simple graceful embellishments of an argument', they were not symbols, allegories or legends; they were representations coincident with the idea expressed;[40] or—as Coleridge put it—'the coincidence of the word with the thought and the thought with the thing'.[41] This is *Logos*, as far as it can be elaborated into descriptive language.

There was, then, in Cambridge during the nineteenth century a strong Platonic element, manifesting itself above all in an incarnational theology. Coleridge definitely influenced

Julius Hare; both thinkers profoundly influenced F. D. Maurice. F. J. A. Hort acknowledged that he learnt much from
Maurice; Westcott, according to his own testimony, learnt
less because he did not wish to impair his own independent
judgment. But his thought, which is Platonic through and
through, belongs to the same *genre*.

This brings us to our final question. Why do we find, in the
last two decades of the nineteenth century, a very similar
incarnationalism, with equally strong Platonic roots, enunci-
ated by a group of Oxford theologians, notably Henry Scott
Holland and Charles Gore, and with them the other Oxford
contributors to that controversial collection of studies on the
Incarnation, *Lux Mundi*, published in 1889? One might expect
to discern a number of common influences together with a
certain amount of cross-fertilization. In actual fact, this
amounts to less than one would suppose. The 'Holy Party' at
Oxford was composed of young High Churchmen who were
the true and natural heirs and successors of Newman, Pusey
and Keble. They owed nothing to F. D. Maurice and very
little to Coleridge. Their formal instruction in Platonism and
Hegelianism came from T. H. Green, whose influence seems
to have been confined to Oxford and made not the slightest
impact on Westcott. Charles Gore clearly shared with Westcott
a profound respect for Origen, from whom his understanding
of the implications of *kenosis* was derived. The only certain
common influence is Robert Browning, saluted by all of them
as the poet of their times, who had somehow found the words
and images to express their feelings with a greater sensitivity
than any other living writer. As for direct cross-fertilization,
it is true that both Gore and Holland had sat at Westcott's feet
at different periods of their lives—Gore as a boy at Harrow,
Holland in studying for ordination with Westcott in 1872.
While specific teaching was absorbed, and acknowledged by
Holland in typically rhapsodic prose, no enduring relationship
was struck up; and although in later years common work for
the Christian Social Union brought all three of them together
again, their association seems never to have been intimate or
to have gone beyond mutual respect. There is no evidence, for
instance, that Westcott ever read *Lux Mundi*. Certainly he did

83

not employ the argument from *kenosis* in his own incarnational writings.*

Charles Gore and Scott Holland owed practically nothing to the Platonic tradition within Cambridge theology. They were Oxford men; and if the mood and temper of their writings were different from those of Newman and his friends, this difference reflects a definite change in Oxford teaching and in Oxford's style. Stedman, for instance, writing in the 1870's, points to a new cult in Oxford—that of 'sweetness and light', its devotees being those 'who believe in Christianity as expounded by Matthew Arnold, ardent lovers of "sweetness and light", turning aside with supercilious pity from the blatant "Philistinism" of the political arena, to meditate over the rhythm of some French essayist and the general prospect of their new religion'.[42] Mr G. R. G. Mure has expressed the same manifestation rather differently. A new Oxford was born with the changes wrought by Jowett in Oxford Greats and the advent of Hegelianism in the last quarter of the century. He describes it as 'the English interpretation of a teutonic idealism, the roots of which go back as far as Socrates. . . . I am certain that without the Platonic Socrates there would have been no Oxford manner.'[43]

There is some truth in both these statements—at least in very general terms. Matthew Arnold, for all his flirtation with obscure French Romantics and his singular attachment to a style which he fondly imagined to be Celtic, was an Oxford man writing for Oxonians. Sometimes he revealed his love for that 'beautiful city . . . adorable dreamer' by mocking its bland parochialism; sometimes he unashamedly appealed to the sentiment of nostalgia, as in *The Scholar-Gipsy*, which made the aged Cardinal Manning—years later—take aside young J. E. C. Bodley and read of 'Godstow Bridge when hay-time's here' and 'the line of festal light in Christ Church hall', saying softly to him 'Ah! only Oxford men like you and me can understand that. . . . Only Oxford men like us.'[44]

Matthew Arnold at Oxford reacted sharply against his liberal, Aristotelian father, while deriving much more from him than he could consciously acknowledge; he was entranced

* The problem of cross-fertilization is discussed more fully in Appendix F.

by Newman, whom he revered all his life, while representing an undogmatic Christianity utterly abhorrent to the man whose good opinion he would most have valued of any man in the world. Perhaps because he was so untypical he was admired by Oxford men, especially the younger men who read *Culture and Anarchy* and the *Essays in Criticism* when they first appeared. It is not difficult to see why. Arnold combined profound sensibility, most particularly to the Oxford *ethos*, with irreverence and flippancy; he wrote in the phrases and cadences which Oxford men loved ever since they first heard them from Newman in the pulpit at St Mary's; and he taught a particular brand of élitism which identified the remnant, the guardians of sweetness and light, with the taste, culture and style most patently found (if indeed found at all in England elsewhere) in Masters of Arts of the University of Oxford.

As good a case could be made out for proving Matthew Arnold to have been an Aristotelian as one could devise for establishing that he was a Platonist.* In this sense (and perhaps in this sense only) he resembled Newman—a man of Platonic temper and disposition who had acquired the training of an Aristotelian. Arnold liked to take the stand of being down to earth, allegedly to see things as they really are (a good Greek attribute, but Arnold did not mean it in a Platonic sense); he had no patience with people who must disguise reality with a sort of *Aberglaube*, the yearning for mysteries usually taking the form of metaphysics or religious dogma. If this yearning had to be satisfied in the past, the modern *Zeitgeist* was dispelling the need for such trappings.[45] This was one side of Matthew Arnold. But while there was a down-to-earthness about him, a severe puritan streak, a gritty realism which enabled this hard-pressed Inspector of Schools to discern the superior elements of continental educational systems, there was also a wistful and romantic side. Arnold was drawn to the contemplative life, almost—one feels—because he was always himself far too busy to enjoy it.

These two sides form both the man and his philosophy. If there must be light, there must also be sweetness; if Hebraism, also Hellenism; if conduct mattered (to the extent of being

* This question is further discussed in Appendix G.

three-fourths of life), so also did style. It was in his lectures as Professor of Poetry that Arnold talked to Oxford men about style—the 'grand style', what it was and what it was not. What it was not (in Arnold's view) was personified in Francis Newman, a pathetic figure of shambling ineffectiveness who had the uncanny knack of saying the wrong thing at the wrong time in the wrong way.[46] Expressed positively, the 'grand style' was that golden moment 'when a noble nature, poetically gifted, treats with simplicity or with severity, a serious subject'.[47] Recognition of it was defined in almost exactly the romantic terms which Coleridge and Newman used to describe faith. It was a quality which could 'only be spiritually discerned'. 'Woe to those who know it not.' 'One must feel it in order to know what it is.'[48] When one goes further, one approaches Newman's idea of the union of logic and rhetoric, thought and expression, and the Aristotelian conception of 'style is the man'. The power of poetry is the union of style and idea. 'One is not enough without the other.' Gautier missed it because he was all style and no ideas; Wordsworth missed it because he had ideas without style to express them.[49] But Sophocles had it, and Milton—for an Englishman—superbly so.[50]

Now this is subtly different from Aristotle's *phronesis*, the quality that denoted right judgment in ethical matters, a sort of intuitive expertise that is manifested in a man of good life; and although Arnold's *beau ideal* was very similar to Aristotle's magnanimous man, he had one quality which was lacking in that other worthy soul. He had charm. He had what Newman had, though not included in Newman's description of the Aristotelian model in the *Idea*. The equivalent of *phronesis* in Arnold, therefore, became a sort of divine, poetic tact which both discerns what is right and apposite and wins all like-minded souls to the same way of thinking by the charm and the sense of magic which it evokes.

Was this, then, a Platonic ingredient which Arnold added? Only in a way which perhaps defies all words to describe. This romantic appeal of Arnold, coming at exactly the time that Plato became general reading in the Oxford Schools, when the *Republic* was put on a par with Aristotle's *Ethics* in the Greats course, fostered a curious romantic brand of Platonism which was already beginning to manifest itself in the Oxford *ethos*. Plato *has* a charm which Aristotle lacks. It may be something to do with the Dialogue form. It certainly has a great deal to do with the character of Socrates. It is bound up with a sense of atmosphere and background, the incomparable setting of such dialogues as the *Charmides*, the *Symposium*, the *Phaedo* and—above all—the *Phaedrus*. Here was philosophy and gentle discourse in a tent, at a feast, on a boat during a poignant and pathetic journey; above all—on the banks of the Ilissus. To anyone who has studied his Greek philosophers the wrong way round, as Oxford men had done, the transition from Aristotle to Plato is like a walk on the open fells after a trudge through a crowded street. Forgive them their exuberance and their intoxication. Who has not, in his heart of hearts, felt the same?

The 'Oxford manner' had, one suspects, as much to do with sweetness and light as with Hegelianism. To be more exact, the Hegelianism, as it was transmitted by T. H. Green, converted the sweet melancholy of Arnold's romanticism into an active and urgent idealism. To the style was added a sense of purpose and the consciousness that life was for action, thus forming a compound which, for want of a better expression, we may call romantic Platonism. It nourished those men of substance who were Jowett's pupils at Balliol, inspired the joyful spirit of the Holy Party, and supplied the *ethos* of that 'old Oxford' the passing of which Max Beerbohm lamented in his preface to *Zuleika Dobson*. It may be recalled that the Duke of Dorset assumed at once the Socratic role when confronted by 'Mr Smith', the average undergraduate, lounging down the steps at the front of Queen's. The foolish fellow didn't know the rules of the game and tried to put questions to the Duke. 'The Socratic manner is not a game at which two can play', the Duke replied. 'Please answer my question, to the best of your ability.'[51]

A sanguine mood and the sanguine philosophy of idealism led in time to a theology expressed in equally sanguine terms—for this is what the incarnationalism of Gore and Holland was all about. The 'Holy Party' at Oxford was composed of young men in the prime of their lives, stimulated by great teachers and bound together as a group of friends with a resolute sense of purpose. Even so their language was extravagant by any standards. They loved Oxford; they loved England ('Was there ever such a country, this side of Paradise?' wrote Holland in *A Bundle of Memories*);[52] they loved each other. 'There was never a shadow upon our joy in being together', Holland wrote of Francis Paget, looking back upon the golden years of the 1870's. '. . . We lived in the glory of flannels and shooting-jackets, climbing, bathing, reading—and always laughing. Life was all unbuttoned . . . there were no invading cares. . . . Nature was on our side; and we were one with it.'[53]

It is hard for us to penetrate this world—a generation of, admittedly, very favoured young men, who felt no brooding sense of cosmic disaster, who had no experience or even memory of the ugliness of war. If the prosperity of mid-Victorian England was shortly to receive a violent jolt, this could not have been anticipated by these ardent young men on the threshold of splendid careers in a country of limitless imperial pretensions and of massive—almost Athenian—national pride. Nature seemed, indeed, to be on their side. We find it all in Holland's florid, nostalgic prose—summers when the sun was always shining; long leisurely days when there was time to savour books and walks beside the river; and if our minds go back at once to the sort of intense, romantic Platonism which William Cory engendered in his pupils at Eton, and beyond that to other days when Socrates talked the long day through with Phaedrus on the banks of the Ilissus, then the association of ideas is no false one.

In short, these were not the times, and this was not the world, of a theology of the Cross. When nature appears to be on our side, then God appears to work through men and through men's achievements. The theology of the *Lux Mundi* group, in so far as it expressed the mood and philosophy of its times, could hardly fail to be a demonstration of the way in which man had been elevated and ennobled by the supreme event of the Incarnation. In such a way does history shape theology.

*   *   *

Plato and Incarnationalism

In Canto I of *Don Juan*, Byron spoke his mind about Platonists:

> Oh Plato! Plato! You have paved the way,
> With your confounded fantasies, to more
> Immoral conduct by the fancied sway
> Your system feigned o'er this controlless core
> Of human hearts, than all the long array
> Of poets and romances: You're a bore,
> A charlatan, a coxcomb—and have been
> At best, no better than a go-between.

One has to sympathize with Byron at times. At least, here, he recognized that Plato's influence was a real one, even if pernicious. Had he lived longer into the nineteenth century his worst fears would have been confirmed. As long as Romanticism lasted, Platonism thrived.

To the historian rash enough to attempt to trace the influence, the references and examples far exceed his power to assimilate or to analyse them. For this reason I have tried to base my enquiry upon an original riddle posed by F. D. Maurice and to see where it would lead me. One question, however, has not been posed; and this for the simple reason that it cannot really be answered. How was this 'fancied sway' of Plato translated into conduct?

This is for others to speculate upon. It is given to few of us to know why we do the things that we do; and it is given to fewer still to supply that answer for characters in the past. The most that an historian of ideas can hope to do is to explain why people thought in the way that they did and to account for an attitude of mind. And since it is the attitude of mind, the predisposition to accept a certain line of thinking and to reject another (Newman's illative sense, perhaps) which so largely determines a person's judgment, then the nearer that we can get to the books that were read and absorbed, the corpus of ideas that was cherished, the better we shall understand the values and ideals of the *literati*, or clerisy, of the particular period under review.

There are, however, moments—'spots of time', perhaps—when the concrete image gives us greater assurance, when the abstraction is for a moment solidified, and we can be certain

89

that what might have seemed a mere acknowledgement was in truth a living passion, or that some particular reflection was being genuinely acted out: the Oxford tutor who rescues his Aristotle from under his pillow; Blake falling upon his knees to pray for inspiration; Shelley rushing out to catechize a mother and child on *anamnesis* while crossing Magdalene Bridge; the boy Wordsworth clutching a five-barred gate until his knuckles turned white to gain conviction of a reality outside himself; Coleridge seeing visions in the fitful flickerings of a dying fire.

At such moments as these, what a person thought becomes truly what that person felt, and a lifeless abstraction has become a living idea. And if this is to speak the language of the Romantics, then no matter: so let it be. In the end they can only be described in their own terms.

Reason and Imagination

Coleridge was very concerned about the meaning of words, as any student of his writings soon discovers to his cost; and the *nuances* and distinctions within his epistemological vocabulary constitute a major problem of interpretation. It is a sad fact that the more conscious a philosopher becomes of the need for clarity, the more technical terms he invents, or the more technical becomes his usage of words which we once thought we understood. Coleridge is the supreme example. It may help to make four general observations about the relationship between Reason and Imagination, as indicated in his writings; but one does so rather tentatively since Coleridge himself was precise in making what we may describe as hierarchical or vertical distinctions—e.g. between Reason and Understanding, and between Imagination and Fancy[1]—but exceedingly vague when it came to lateral or horizontal distinctions, such as the relationship between the philosophical quality of Reason and the poetical attribute of Imagination.

In the first place, it could be argued that there is virtually no distinction at all. Coleridge grew from the one concept into the other. There is no doubt that his preoccupation with the Imagination declined as his own interests moved from the sphere of poetic truth to that of philosophy and theology. It is true that the transition took a long time to accomplish and that for a while it is impossible to say which interest was uppermost in his mind. But by 1815, when the *Biographia Literaria* was published, Coleridge had in fact said his last word about Imagination, whereas the classic exposition on the distinction between Reason and Understanding, which was being worked out in the years that he was writing *The Friend*, was made in 1825 with the publication of *Aids to Reflection*. It may be said, then, that Reason took over within the sphere of philosophy and theology what Imagination had served to illuminate within the sphere of aesthetics and poetry.

Appendix A

Secondly, it is significant that the gradual change in vocabulary was marked by Coleridge's increasing interest in German thought and the writings of the seventeenth-century divines within the Platonic tradition. Both these interests had been exhibited at an early stage and might seem to have been at their height at the turn of the century, following Coleridge's first study of the German language and his visit to Germany in 1798/9. It could be argued, too, that Coleridge's terminology for poetical inspiration was as much shaped by his acquaintance with the writing of Kant and Schelling as was his later philosophical language.[2] But this is not quite the point. Two considerations have to be borne in mind here. The first is the fact that Coleridge came more and more to see, through the writings of the seventeenth-century divines, that 'reason' as the *Aufklärung* had defined it needed to be put into the proper relationship with the quality which the Platonists described as 'higher reason' or the intuitive faculty, and that therefore the epistemological battle had really to be fought out within these terms.[3] Secondly, as Mr McFarland has shown in the study of *Coleridge and the Pantheist Tradition*, one could not get away from Kant. Although he may not have invented the distinction between Reason and Understanding, Kant had exercised so paramount an influence, that all his disciples and critics had either to complete or to refute his system by occupying the same ground. What had emerged was a common philosophical vocabulary, which all thinkers had perforce to use—a point to be remembered, incidentally, when discussing the frequent accusations of plagiarism which were levelled at practically every post-Kantian philosopher, and notably at Coleridge himself.[4]

The third general observation is this: Reason and Imagination—in Coleridge's writings—are in a sense parallel modes of cognition, partaking of very similar characteristics, the chief of these being the realization that the higher cognitive powers necessarily subsume the lower. Fancy may be inferior to Imagination, but it is a part of the higher faculty. In the same way, Understanding is not eliminated from Reason. It may operate in a different way, by judging purely according to senses, but it is a part of a higher process and not cancelled out by being superseded. Examples abound from Coleridge's writings, but this passage from the *Aids to Reflection* has been chosen because it expresses Coleridge's own position so succinctly, while revealing well his debt to Kant, whose definition of *a priori* reasoning he has manifestly in mind:

The reason supersedes the whole process, and on the first conception presented by the understanding in consequence of the first sight of a triangular figure, of whatever sort it might chance to be, it affirms with an assurance incapable of future increase, with a perfect certainty, that in all possible triangles any two of the enclosing lines will and must be greater than the third. In short, understanding in its highest form of experience remains commensurate with the experimental notices of the senses from which it is generalised. Reason, on the other hand, either predetermines experience, or avails itself of a past experience to supersede its necessity in all future time; and affirms truths which no sense could perceive, nor experiment verify, nor experience confirm.[5]

The fourth point arises from this last one. Neither Reason nor Imagination could be conceived as a single faculty appropriate to one particular organ of the body or the mind. It is not, for instance, true to say that we imagine in our hearts, understand from what we see with our eyes and reason in our minds, though this functional relationship is not so very far from the truth. From what has been said earlier it must be clear that since Reason subsumes all the lower faculties, it must itself be a total process involving all the faculties. There must be a union of thought and feeling. Coleridge defined his whole life's work in these terms; 'to support all old and venerable truths, to support, to kindle, to project, to make the reason spread light over our feelings, to make our feelings diffuse vital warmth through our reason'.[6] Miss Snyder has commented on this:

There resulted a vivid realisation of the extent to which all thinking is determined by assumptions, ideas, images, and attitudes of ever less tangible sorts. Coleridge's insistence that fertile thinking involved more than induction, and experience more than what it commonly meant to empiricists; that the premisses are the critical part of reasoning, and that they depend on something other than the understanding—as a power that brings into play the total man—these principles of thought and method were formulated through his contacts with many philosophic minds, but to no small extent through their use in the physiological and chemical controversies in which he took part.[7]

This point alone should make us very chary of pressing a distinction between Reason and Imagination, when they were so closely associated in Coleridge's own mind.

Antinomies, Contradictions
and Contraries

In the third lecture, the point was made that the drift of Plato's teaching in the *Theaetetus*, the *Parmenides* and the *Sophist* is towards a position which could not admit as knowledge an argument which concluded in a fundamental contradiction. Nor, as is well known, could Immanuel Kant, in formulating his concept of antinomies. In the *Critique of Pure Reason* he made short work of the problem posed in the *Parmenides* by exposing the contradiction that the universe can be both in motion and at rest as an argument proceeding from false definitions.[1] But even if the logic had been superior, the results may still be no more than an antinomy. One may supply convincing proofs to support contradictory contentions (as Kant did with his four antinomies of pure reason), but the antinomy itself is not the enunciation of some higher truth, but rather the demonstration of an affliction of human understanding.

> Since the arguments on both sides are equally clear, it is impossible to decide between them. The parties may be commanded to keep the peace before the tribunal of reason: but the controversy nevertheless continues. There can therefore be no way of settling once and for all to the satisfaction of both sides, save by their becoming convinced that the very fact of their being able so admirably to refute one another is evidence that they are really quarrelling about nothing, and that a certain transcendental illusion has mocked them with a reality where none is to be found.[2]

Here it would be well to define our terms. A contradiction and an antinomy may amount to the same thing, but they are not exactly the same in meaning. A contradiction is the point where two different predicates are made to occupy the same predicative position so that the result is an absurdity, a logical monstrosity. One of the

95

positions *must* be true, the other therefore cannot be. An antinomy—such as the conclusion from a logical argument that the world has a beginning in time, countered by an equally logical argument that it has no beginning—is a *prima facie* contradiction, but it may not actually be so since it is related to a type of problem which may not be knowable. While we can say of an antinomy that one or the other conclusion must be true, and therefore one or the other must be false, we can also say of it that *either* in coming to this logical impasse we have exceeded the bounds of human knowledge (as Kant was to suggest in his *Critique*) *or* that because we have reached this apparent impasse, there must be some higher reason which resolves it (the answer given by Hegel).[3]

As for contradictions themselves, there was a tradition going back to Aristotle (and possibly derived by Aristotle from Plato himself) that a contradictory antithesis is not the same as a contrary antithesis. The contradictory antithesis was defined by Aristotle as an opposition in both quantity and quality; the contrary antithesis as a condition where both propositions were universal while opposed in quality only.[4] Most of the Romantics employed this distinction, although not always meaning the same thing by it; some with actual reference to Kant's theory of antinomies, others as an expression of a metaphysical concept rather than a logical process.

Hegel appears to have been the exception; not because he was content to leave Kant's enigma of the antinomies where he found it, but for the opposite reason. While Kant dismissed the *Parmenides*, Hegel regarded it as 'the true uncovering and positive expression of the Divine Life'.[5] Because he believed that Kant 'never got beyond the negative result that the thing—in—itself is unknowable'[6] and failed to perceive that 'the phenomenal world is not the terminus of thought'; that 'there is another and higher region', erroneously considered by Kant as an 'inaccessible "other world" ',[7] Hegel regarded all contradictions themselves as reconciled within the sphere of the Absolute. In this way Hegel puzzled his contemporaries and bewildered posterity by using the logical term 'contradiction' to apply to an order of existence (the Absolute) for which only metaphysical language could properly apply. It is fair to say that not all Hegel's interpreters have agreed as to the way in which these contradictions *can* be reconciled. Walter Kaufmann, for instance, tones down Hegel's notion of the Absolute, throwing the

burden of Hegel's criticism of Kant onto the seemingly sounder
argument that Kant created his own antinomies by an imperfect
definition of his categories.[8] Mr G. R. G. Mure, on the other hand,
stresses Hegel's appreciation of different levels of thinking, praising
him for his ingenuity in delivering the thought of his time from the
paralysing effect of the law of contradictions by the dynamic theory
that 'identity in difference always betokens development, and vice-
versa. . . . If identity in difference and development be totally denied,
all inference is either invalid or *petitio principii*. Even the so-called
"implication" of the Logisticians is an unacknowledged ghost of
identity in difference.'[9]

Coleridge could use this language, but he was both more respectful
to Kant and much more careful to make the distinction between
possible and impossible antitheses. Both he and Blake before him
somewhat confused the issue, however, by inventing their own
terminology. To Blake, for instance, the fundamental distinction
was between 'contraries' and 'negations'. At the beginning of Book
Two of *Milton*, we are told:

> Contraries are positives
> A Negation is not a contrary.[10]

In *Jerusalem*, the 'manner of the Sons of Albion in their strength'
is described thus:

> They take the Two Contraries which are call'd Qualities,
>   with which
> Every Substance is clothed: they name them Good and Evil
> From them they make an Abstract, which is a Negation
> Not only of the Substance from which it is derived,
> A murderer of its own Body, but also a murderer
> Of every Divine Member; it is the Reasoning Power,
> An Abstract objecting power that Negatives everything.[11]

There is, of course, nothing of Kant in all this; but plenty of Plato,
or at least the Neoplatonic tradition, as will be seen later. Blake was
not interested in the terminology of logic or philosophy, save to
imply that it all belonged to the 'Reasoning Power' which is
negating anyway; but we have to employ philosophical terms to
explain the distinction. Contraries were the essential elements
within the dialectic of life, the two polar positions constantly in

97

tension, creating the movement or 'progression' within the world. The one might be good, the other bad; but at least they were positive qualities engendering an opposite force. Negations, on the other hand, were dead things—grey, intermediate, nonentities, which had no opposites, strictly speaking, because they possessed no qualities to bring the opposite forces into being. A Negation, then is not really a contradiction; or if so, it is more a contradiction to the principle of life itself, because it is lifeless and inert within a dynamic world.

Coleridge was both more explicit and more philosophical. There were two forms of antithesis or opposition. The first, he described in the *Biographia Literaria* as 'logical and incompatible', using the Eleatic enigma of a body at once at rest and in motion as his example. This was a contradiction and, as such, irreconcilable.[12] As he explained in *The Friend*, again using a Socratic example, certain contraries cannot be reconciled: black cannot be white, two straight lines can never include a square.[13] This form of opposite he describes as a 'contrary', meaning by the word something very different from Blake's usage.[14] He means, as he wrote in a notebook entry, 'Negative Quantities' as distinguished from 'opposed forces'.

> Logical by Contradiction ends in absolute nothing, nihil *negativum* quod est etiam irrepresentabile—a ball in motion and at the same time not in motion, motion in each sentence having been used in the same sense, is a contradiction in terms/in Nature it is *not*, or rather say, it isn't, so as not to give a moment's reality by the use of the word per se, *is*.

There was, however, a second form of antithesis, which he was wont to describe as an 'opposite' rather than a 'contrary'. 'But there are oppositions without contradiction', he continued in his notebook, 'and *real*—nihil privativum cogitabile—two tendencies to motion in the same body, one to N. other to S., being equipollent, the Body remains *in rest*—the second assumed Tendency is a real negative Quantity—better therefore called, a *privative* Quantity.-4 $-5 =$ -9 is mere pedantry—there is no real *sub*traction/it is true *addition*. $-$ and $+$ have no meanings but as symbols of opposition.'[15] Again, in the *Biographia Literaria*, he described this second antithesis as 'real, without being contradictory'.[16] One of the chief errors of the world was to confuse these two forms of antithesis, to see all

forms of opposition as contradiction, in short to fail to distinguish
between a 'contrary' and an 'opposite'. Southey, he thought, fell too
often into this trap. Among Coleridge's marginalia to Baxter's *Life of
Himself*, we find this observation:

> S. [Southey] saw all differences as Diversity, while I am striving
> to reduce supposed Contraries into compatible Opposites, whose
> worst errors consisted in their reciprocal Exclusion of each other.
> So S. found positive falsehoods where I saw half-truths, and found
> the falsehood in the partial Eclipse. S = a Grey hound. S.T.C. =
> a Pointer.[17]

Coleridge's fullest description of the difference between 'contraries' and 'opposites' may be found, however, in his essay *On
the Constitution of the Church and State*:

> Let me call attention [he writes] to the essential difference be-
> tween 'opposite' and 'contrary'. Opposite powers are always of
> the same kind, and tend to union, either by equipoise or by a
> common product. Thus the + and − poles of the magnet, thus
> positive and negative electricity, are opposites. Sweet and sour
> are opposites; sweet and bitter are contraries. The feminine
> character is opposed to the masculine; but the effeminate is its
> contrary. Even so in the present instance, the interest of per-
> manence is opposed to that of progressiveness; but so far from
> being contrary interests, they, like magnetic forces, suppose and
> require each other.[18]

The important point—he observes later—is that 'polar forces—
that is, opposite, not contrary, powers—are necessarily *unius generis*,
homogeneous'.[19] While split, or divided, they have the tendency to
reunion within them, because the one opposite has been generated
from the other. This, he says in *The Idea of the Christian Church* is 'an
old rule of logic'. 'Antagonist forces are necessarily of the same
kind. . . . *Inter res heterogeneas non datur oppositio*: that is, contraries
cannot be opposites. Alike in the primary and the metaphorical use
of the word, rivals (*rivales*) are those only who inhabit the opposite
banks of the same stream.'[20]

APPENDIX C

Coleridge's 'Trichotomous Logic'

So fascinated was Coleridge by oppositions which were really no oppositions, and by apparent opposites which were at some higher or transcendent stage reconciled, that he did not very carefully distinguish between them. The main distinction to bear in mind, however, is that between the Aristotelian triad and the dialectical triad.

The Aristotelian triad is not really a reconciliation of opposites at all. It is rather a reduction of certain elements in the extreme positions in order to attain a mean. According to the *Nicomachean Ethics*, virtue exists in a condition which is a mid-point between two poles, one of which is an excess of the quality and the other a corresponding deficiency. 'We call it a mean condition as lying between two forms of badness,' Aristotle writes, 'one being excess and the other deficiency.'[1] Thus between the two poles of foolhardiness and cowardice lies the mean position of courage; between the poles of prodigality and meanness, is the middle virtue of 'liberality'.[2] 'Goodness', Aristotle says in the *Politics*, 'consists in a mean.'[3] Now this is not what Coleridge meant when he used the term 'Extremes meet', although occasionally he gives an example of such a reconciliation of opposites which turns out to be an Aristotelian triad. This is sometimes because his dialectical triad is an imperfect one, i.e. his third position is a mesothesis not a synthesis; sometimes because in his admission that two extreme evil positions cannot be reconciled into a good, the only good that can be expressed in a triadic form must be a mean position in which the evil aspect of both poles has been eradicated. In the *Aids to Reflection*, for instance, Coleridge praises the Church of England for avoiding two errors at the poles—'ultra-fidianism' at the one pole and 'minimi-fidianism' at the other.[4]

This is a perfect example of an Aristotelian triad; and a footnote in the same work—'Extremes appear to generate each other; but if we look steadily, there will most often be found some common error, that produces both as its positive and negative poles'[5]—suggests that Coleridge was well aware of it. Again, in the *Constitution of Church and State*, he makes the point that the constitutional virtue of parliamentary omnipotence is the mean between two poles—'a democratic republic and an absolute monarchy'—which reflect well the adage of 'Extremes meet' since 'in both alike, the nation or people delegates its whole power'.[6] He puts a very similar argument in *The Friend* when discussing the resemblances, at the extremes, of aristocratic despotism and despotic Jacobinism.[7] A sound constitutional principle has been perverted by an excess of a quality at one pole and its defect at the other, which extreme positions produce exactly the same evil result. In the *Lay Sermons*, Coleridge praises the quality of reverent inquiry with regard to scriptural revelation as opposed to the two poles of scepticism (an excess of the inquiring spirit) and superstition (a defect of it).[8] He then goes on, with a very Aristotelian observation: 'To expose the inconsistency of both these extremes, and by inference to recommend that state of mind, which looks forward *to the fellowship of the mystery of the faith as a spirit of wisdom and revelation* in the knowledge of *God, the eyes of* the understanding *being enlightened* (Eph. 1.17, 18)—this formed my general purpose.'[9] Two evils cannot be reconciled into a good without a reduction. In the *Table Talk* he is recorded as saying: 'We do not win heaven by logic. Unitarianism is, in effect, the worst of one kind of Atheism, joined to the worst of one kind of Calvinism, like two asses tied tail to tail.'[10]

The dialectical triad, which was Coleridge's explanation in logical terms of the reconciliation of opposites, was what he had in mind in the use of the word 'trichotomy'. Professor Muirhead has given an excellent account of its working.

> Instead of starting with opposing concepts [he writes], in one or other of which, taken separately we are to find the truth, we have to 'seek first for the Unity as the only source of Reality, and then for the two opposites yet correspondent forms by which it manifests itself. For it is an axiom of universal application that *manifestatio non datur nisi per alterum*. Instead therefore of affirmation and contradiction, the tools of dichotamic logic, we have three terms Identity, Thesis and Antithesis.' It is on this principle that he

Appendix C

[Coleridge] conceived it possible to advance beyond the limitations of Logic or the science of the Understanding to a Noetic, or science of the Reason, which should also be a science of Reality.[11]

Now had Coleridge ever had the power and will to produce his *magnum opus*, the *Organon vere Organum*, doubtless a full exposition of trichotomous logic would have been supplied, together with its history. Even so, a great many references and fragments have survived to enable us to gain a fair idea of what he meant. From Bruno (he tells us), he derived the principle; from Richard Baxter, the true nature of the method.

There seems little doubt (in view of Mr Owen Barfield's recent researches) that he was wrong about Bruno. He read the idea of polar logic into his writings, so indulging in the Coleridgean practice of modifying the thought of a previous thinker 'in the process of adapting it to his own'.[12] Nevertheless what Coleridge actually ascribed to Bruno was as follows—the 'polar principle—that is that in order to manifest itself every power must appear in two opposites, but these two opposites having a ground of identity were constantly striving to reunite, but not being permitted to pass back to their organic state, which would amount to annihilation, they pressed forward and the two formed a third something'.[13] Here, then, is the triad—the two poles of thesis and antithesis, and a 'higher third' which was the Identity of the two. This appears to be so similar to the *Identität philosophie* of Schelling and the dialectic of Hegel as to be barely distinguishable. The sense of dynamic is there in the tension or reciprocity between the polar opposites and the reconciliation, or Identity, whereby subject and object become one, or as Schelling put it, when 'the perceiving or intuiting self is identical with that which he perceives'.[14] But Coleridge not only arrived at this dialectic independently of Schelling, he derived his method from a source unknown to the Germans, namely Richard Baxter's *Methodus Theologia*. It is difficult to see, when reading Coleridge's comments on Baxter, what it was he found that was such a revelation. Even he admitted that Baxter's treatment of trichotomy was little more than a conjunction of the Polar Logic of Bruno and the Pythagorean *tetractys*. The peculiar genius of Baxter was to have an insight into the nature of dialectic which appeared to have been denied to Kant. While Kant had substituted the terminology of trichotomy—

'thesis, antithesis, synthesis'—for the old logic of dichotomy, which had failed to see the distinction between an opposite and a contrary, he had not recognized the power of the tool that he had in his hands. Baxter, on the other hand, he writes—'grounded the necessity of Trichotomy, as the Principle of Real Logic, on an absolute Idea presupposed in all intelligential Acts; whereas Kant adopts it merely as a fact of Reflection, tho' doubtless as a singular and curious Fact in which he suspects some yet deeper Truth latent and hereafter to be discovered'.[15]

The 'higher third' or the Identity is the point of reconciliation of the two poles. But to render the matter more complex, Coleridge frequently employed more figures than three, sometimes setting out his position as a pentad, occasionally as a heptad, and based them all on the mystical Pythagorean symbol of the *tetractys*, a triangular figure of ten points, rising from a base of four,[16] the whole representing the Supreme Being. The origins and significance of these various figures, bringing us into the puzzling world of number-symbolism, need not detain us. Certainly Coleridge was very familiar with the Pythagorean tradition and with the writings of the Neoplatonists, especially Iamblichus and Proclus, who elaborated the Platonic dialectic into series of triads, all attempting to express the procession of a divisible whole from an indivisible whole,[17] which was exactly the problem posed by Coleridge when he worked from the principle of unity to the division into two polar opposites. The pentad was the figure which Coleridge most frequently employed, and this was built up on geometrical premisses.

The five figures are as follows. At two poles of a straight horizontal line are *thesis* and *antithesis*, standing for subject and object, or positive and negative. At the centre of the line that divides them is the equatorial point, being equidistant from both thesis and antithesis. This is called the *mesothesis*, or point of indifference. This is a difficult term to understand. It is not the identity of the two poles; but when viewed from either one of the poles it will partake of the characteristic of the other. It is both poles, but in different relations. A perfect example occurs in the *Phaedo*. When it is pointed out that Simmias may be bigger than Socrates but smaller than Phaedo, it would not be correct to predicate of Simmias both greatness and smallness. He is only relatively tall or short, according to whether he is looked at by Socrates or by Phaedo. In that sense, Simmias is the mesothesis, or *punctum indifferens* between the small Socrates and the large Phaedo.[18] But there is another sense in which the *mesothesis* is the mean between the two poles. Coleridge explains as follows:

> When two objects, that stand to each other in the relation of anti-thesis or contradistinction, are connected by a middle term common to both, the sense of this middle term is indifferently determinable by either; the preferability of the one or the other in any given case being divided by the circumstance of our more frequent experience of, or greater familiarity with, the term in this connection. Thus, if I put hydrogen and oxygen gas, as opposite poles, the term gas is common to both, and it is a matter of indifference by which of the two bodies I ascertain the sense of the term.[19]

If one were to draw a vertical line through the equatorial point, then two more poles would come into being, thus making the five figures. In addition to the thesis, antithesis, and mesothesis on the horizontal, you have the two poles on the vertical, called respectively *prothesis*, at the top, and *synthesis* at the bottom. The completed pentad thus becomes a *quincunx*, as follows:

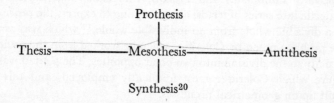

```
                    Prothesis
                        |
                        |
Thesis————————————Mesothesis————————————Antithesis
                        |
                        |
                    Synthesis[20]
```

Coleridge described the *prothesis* as the *coherence* of thesis and antithesis; the *synthesis* as *composition* (or equilibrium). A more explicit comparison occurs in his 'Essay on Faith', published in the fourth volume of the *Literary Remains*.

> Synthesis [he writes] is a putting together of the two [thesis and antithesis], so that a third something is generated. Thus the *synthesis* of hydrogen and oxygen is water, a third something, neither hydrogen nor oxygen. But the blade of a knife and its handle when put together do not form a *synthesis*, but still remain a blade and a handle. And as a *synthesis* is a unity that results from the union of two things, so a prothesis is a primary unity that gives itself forth into two things.[21]

The prothesis is the Higher Third. But in its absolute meaning it is the One, the Supreme Being, the apex, the tetractys, and this it must be because it is the total idea in which subject and object are really one. It is the idea of absolute identity of the two, as existed from the first. The *synthesis* is the actual interconnection or copula of the two, merging them into one. This composition as opposed to coherence may not mean that synthesis is identical on a finite level with prothesis in the realm of the absolute. In Coleridge's 'Heptad of colours', for instance, the figure becomes as follows:

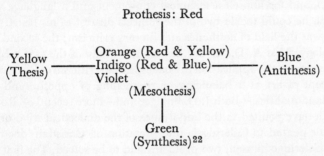

When Coleridge reduces a pentad to a tetrad, he omits the meso-thesis;[23] in a triad, the synthesis holds the only position of identity, and 'the Prothesis takes the name and place of the Thesis—a rule observed in classification generally and as it were constructively'.[24] That it does this, its name implies; and understandably so, because the one and the truly Real would not need to generate an opposite as a condition of its existence, and must be both more subject than object, and more positive than negative. In application, the third figure in a Coleridgean triad sometimes appears to assume the function and nature of both prothesis and synthesis. A triad is referred to, for instance, in the Essay *On the Constitution of Church and State* in connection with the famous distinction between the three estates. The first estate stands for 'permanency'; the second for 'progressiveness'. Here are a thesis and an antithesis. The third estate is the Clerisy which stands for 'cultivation'—described as 'the ground, the necessary antecedent condition, of both the former'.[25] So the third estate is undoubtedly the higher third, because it embraces both the poles. But its nature, described as 'the ground' and 'antecedent' suggests that it is the prothesis; while its function—that of supplying balance or equilibrium—suggests that it is a synthesis. Another example of this ambiguity appears in the same work. Describing the relation of the State to the national Church, Coleridge writes: 'these are two poles of the same magnet; the magnet itself, which is constituted by them, is the constitution of the nation'.[26] That is to say, it is the synthesis, that which provides the essential equipoise; but it might also be represented as the prothesis, since it is the *first* condition from which the poles appear to emanate.

The significance of this law of polarity was really this: Coleridge had found for himself a technical equipment and a language with which he could tackle two of the subjects dearest to his heart. The first was the field of aesthetics and literary criticism; the second was theology. Miss A. D. Snyder has made a study of the first subject, in particular the application to Shakespearian criticism of Coleridge's concept of art as a balancing or reconciling of opposite and discordant qualities.[27] Both J. D. Boulger and—more recently—Robert Barth have pointed to the importance of the dialectical triad or the Neotic pentad to Coleridge's interpretation of Christian doctrine. For Coleridge himself, two problems had to be solved. The first was the task of reconciling his own dynamic philosophy with Christian theology: the second was to apply this dynamic philosophy to the central mystery of the Christian Faith, with which he had himself been preoccupied since his own conversion from the errors of Unitarianism, namely—the doctrine of the Trinity.

The Confessions of an Inquiring Spirit open with a pentad, described by Coleridge as 'The Pentad of Operative Christianity'. The figure is as follows:

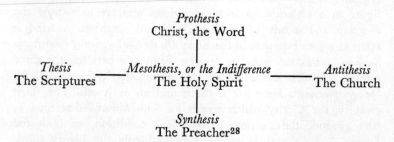

Prothesis
Christ, the Word

|

Thesis ——— *Mesothesis, or the Indifference* ——— *Antithesis*
The Scriptures   The Holy Spirit   The Church

|

Synthesis
The Preacher[28]

To arrive at this, however, Coleridge's argument had been built up by a series of polar opposites, working from the concept of man to that of the Godhead itself. The first polarity was between Nature and

Spirit. This was the fundamental antithesis within the universe, and just as the whole, the universe itself, embraces these opposites in equilibrium (the synthesis), so is this tension reflected in man, the microcosm of the world.[29] There is a natural man and a spiritual man, both combined in Man himself. So, too, is the fundamental polarity reflected in the tension between the Christian Church and the World, not in the dualistic Augustinian sense of the two cities, but with the implication that the subject must express itself in the object and achieve a reconciliation into a higher third which is the world in both its natural and spiritual aspects.[30] Now, taking the phenomenon of Religion itself, a tension between polar opposites can be discerned here. In the seventh letter of *Confessions of an Inquiring Spirit*, the poles are represented as 'subjective, or spiritual and individual' as against the 'objective, or historic and ecclesiastical'. Religion is at one and the same time 'inward Life and Truth, and outward Fact and Luminary'.[31] Or, as Coleridge put it in *The Friend*:

> Religion herself, through her sacred oracles, answers for me, that all effective faith presupposes knowledge and individual conviction. . . . Not that knowledge can of itself do all! The light of religion is not that of the moon, light without heat; but neither is its warmth that of the stove, warmth without light. Religion is the Sun, whose warmth indeed swells, and stirs, and activates the life of nature, but who at the same time beholds all the growth of life with a master-eye, makes all objects glorious on which it looks, and by that glory visible to all others.[32]

If this is so, then one's act of commitment to religion must involve two poles. One receives the historical assurance from the revelation; but this must so affect the individual that he takes that revelation as it concerns him as a moral and responsible person. An act of faith is itself a fusion of two poles. Revelation must have assured that act of faith, Coleridge says: but again, 'my conscience required it'.[33] Faith is something that affirms, but also something that is affirmed. 'It is an eternal and infinite self-rejoicing, self-loving, with a joy unfathomable, with a love all comprehensive. It is absolute; and the absolute is neither singly that which affirms, nor that which is affirmed; but the identity and living copula of both.'[34]

This brings us to the will itself—the relation of the individual to the Absolute Will, and the degree of freedom in that individual to fall into sin or to choose the way of salvation. Here Coleridge introduces the mesothesis into his logical figure. The positive pole is represented as 'actual good', the negative pole as 'potential evil', with the Self as 'the point of indifference between each'. How this came about was the subject of some lengthy musing by Coleridge in one of his notebooks. The fact that 'the Potential must have no longer been the *base*, the latent *ground* of the Actual' and that man found himself in a neutral position with regard to the two poles, must have been the result of the Fall. Time was when 'the individual will remained in harmony with the Absolute Will'. When 'the will realised the negative potency, willed itself individual', then it 'fell into apostasy and Original Sin'.[35] One would expect Coleridge to be entranced by the paradox that 'service is perfect freedom'. Following from this, he appreciated that disobedience against the righteous must be absolute enslavement, the negation of freedom; and yet man is responsible himself for his loss of freedom, because to divest himself of his own freedom in the face of temptation was his own act.[36]

The self was a moral agent: of that Coleridge never had any doubts. His *Confessio Fidei* of 1816 begins with the words—'I BELIEVE that I am a free agent, inasmuch as, and so far as, I have a will, which renders me justly responsible for my actions, omissive as well commissive.'[37] To him the guarantee of that free agency of the moral being as well as of 'the reality of external nature' was the Trinity.[38] It was the mightiest of paradoxes, only to be penetrated by Reason through the process of Noetic logic. The seventeenth-century divines—Bull and Waterland, in particular—had shown the way. The tetrad was expressed thus:

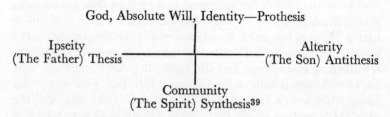

God, Absolute Will, Identity—Prothesis

Ipseity   Alterity
(The Father) Thesis   (The Son) Antithesis

Community
(The Spirit) Synthesis[39]

This tetrad, perhaps, shows the working of the Noetic logic more clearly than any other. *Prothesis* is the Absolute, the Good, the indivisible. 'Ipseity' or the thesis conveys the sense of 'self-sameness', both self-affirming and self-affirmed. But to have expression, there must be an outpouring, the Logos or supreme reason, this standing to the Father as the objective to the subjective, as the antithesis to the thesis. The copula of the two is the life-giving Spirit, expressed in the word Community, reflecting as the base of the vertical line the coherence of Father and Son in the prothesis or Absolute. In Coleridge's definition, it would appear to embrace the mesothesis or equatorial point between Ipseity and Alterity, because it stands 'relatively to the Father, the Spirit of Holiness, the Holy Spirit; relatively to the Son, the Spirit of Truth, whose attribute is Wisdom; *sancta sophia*; the Good or the reality of the True, in the form of actual Life'.[40]

There might seem to be two heterodox elements in this exposition of the Trinity. The first is that Coleridge was exhibiting Father and Son as thesis and antithesis, as two opposite poles, and so encouraging speculation arising from the universal law of being that everything must generate its own opposite in order to exist. Coleridge was, however, careful to safeguard the ways in which 'being' could be predicated of the Father and the Son, using language—as J. D. Boulger points out—strikingly similar to the Scholastic doctrine of *analogia entis*.

Alterity contains the *form* of its own reality, and though one with yet not the same as the form of the *Idem*. Instead of the word *Alter* and *Idem* let us place A = B and B = A; and we then explain our further meaning by saying that B is in A in another sense that A is in B. B is affirmed in A; A is presumed in B; or A *Being*, B co-eternally *becomes*.[41]

The second is the point raised by Professor Shedd, which does indeed expose the weak link in Coleridge's argument. Coleridge appears to assume that the Trinity is grounded on some earlier or 'aboriginal Unity' which had existed primarily by itself (i.e. the prothesis); and this suggests 'a process of development . . . which is incompatible with . . . immutable perfection, and with that golden position of the schoolmen that God is *actus purissimus sine ulla potentialite*.[42] If one introduces into the Godhead any concept of potentiality, then the way is open for pantheism or modalism.

Now it cannot be said that this ingenious logic and all this talk

Appendix C

about 'Ipseity', 'Alterity' and the like had any great influence on the exposition of Trinitarian doctrine in the nineteenth century. Nor was it worked out for this purpose, for Coleridge was chiefly concerned with resolving a dilemma in his own mind. But the dialectical process is of major importance, for the following reason—Coleridge's concept of dialectic was different from Hegel's. Although his use of the term *prothesis* might suggest an affinity with Hegel's realm of infinite essence which is the absolute ground of everything and the explanation of the identity of Being and Thought,[43] Coleridge was more concerned with showing that the existence of pairs of opposites was a necessary condition of life, and that the synthesis, which was the copula or equilibrium between the two did not eradicate or gradually render unnecessary the independent existence of the thesis and the antithesis. The function that the synthesis performed was rather to keep the balance between them, for each was necessary for the other's existence. Although the synthesis might express the identity of thesis and antithesis, it did not diminish the identity of either one or the other. In this way, his theory of polarity was very similar to Blake's. Blake had criticized Swedenborg for his tendency 'to make one Family of Contraries';[44] He was less concerned with the task of reconciling opposites than declaring their coincidence. The truth to Blake was indeed 'Yes *and* No, but neither'.

Further Aspects of
F. D. Maurice's Platonism

The concept of the polarity of truth was not the whole of F. D. Maurice's Platonism; but rather that aspect of Platonism, or a particular interpretation of the tradition, which he derived from Julius Hare and Coleridge. In a wider sense than this, however, has his theology been described as Platonic. As is well known, Maurice's theology was rooted in his interpretation of the Redemption as an act which, having taken place at a particular moment in time, established a new relationship between man and God. Faith consisted in the recognition of that new status, which being divinely ordained, could not be upset or overturned by the blindness of men. We are all God's sons; failure to recognize the fact does not make us any less the Sons of God, because the omnipotence of God cannot be qualified or challenged by the wilfulness of man. As that good Mauricean, R. H. Hutton, put it in his essay on 'The Moral Significance of Atheism', since 'human trust does not create God . . . human distrust would not annihilate Him'.[1] Theology, therefore, is the study of the divine order which God has set up; not what He is building for us; but what He accomplished or proclaimed through the Redemption upon the Cross. The theologian, then, is not so much concerned with an end, a *telos*, to which either revelation is pointing, or the institution of the Church is moving, but with uncovering the edifice which God built in the past and which, being perfect at the time that it was constructed, is perfect still. The theologian is not a speculator; he does not build; he is—more properly—a 'digger', whose main task is to remove the deposits of ignorance and blindness which have covered over the eternal truths and the divine order given to us from the beginning.

It is normally argued that Maurice derived this teaching—a form of 'realized eschatology'—from the writings of the learned Scottish

Arminian, Thomas Erskine of Linlathen.[2] Indeed the fact that
Erskine in the *Brazen Serpent* presented such a view of the Atonement
is beyond dispute; and Maurice certainly read Erskine with the
deepest interest. He learned from him, for instance, an interpretation of the Atonement which enabled him to reject the particularly
crude and repulsive Evangelical eschatology of the day and to
represent the divine sacrifice not as an event demanded by the
requirements of retributive justice, but as an act of saving love.[3]
Christ dies to free man from sin not to free him from the punishment
for sin. And Maurice's conviction that a Covenant between God and
man was established by the Redemption, and the Kingdom of
Christ accordingly set up, was confirmed by his less openly-admitted
admiration for the writings of the millenarianist, Joseph Stephenson,
Rector of Lympsham.[4]

It has not, however, been sufficiently stressed that Maurice could
have found the germ of this teaching in the *Aids to Reflection*. In a
footnote to Aphorism XVIII in the section 'On Spiritual Religion',
we find this remarkable passage:

> *God manifested in the flesh* is eternity in the form of time. But
> eternity in relation to time is as the absolute to the conditional,
> as the real to the apparent, and Redemption must partake of
> both;—always perfected, for it is a *Fiat* of the Eternal;—con-
> tinuous, for it is a process in relation to man; the former the alone
> objectively, and therefore universally, true. That Redemption is an
> *opus perfectum*, a finished work, the claim to which is conferred
> in Baptism: that a Christian cannot speak or think as if his re-
> demption by the blood, and his justification by the righteousness
> of Christ alone, were future or contingent events, but must both say
> and think, I have been redeemed, I am justified, . . .—these are
> truths, which all the Reformed Churches . . .—nay, the best and
> most learned divines of the Roman Catholic Church have united
> in upholding as most certain and necessary articles of faith.[5]

The Redemption is an *opus perfectum*. What God has accomplished,
no man can alter. It was in Maurice's insistence on this that another
and most important element of his Platonism can be discerned. To
Plato, the world of universals is the order of eternity. Men may not
perceive reality in their blindness, or in their delusion that the
objects before their eyes have more reality than the shadows that

they actually are. The philosopher does not create a new world to redress the deficiencies of the old. He helps the ignorant to recognize what the true order was and is, and ever will be. The Platonic philosopher, then, is a 'digger' too, not a builder. F. D. Maurice translated this concept to the sphere of theology and the function of the theologian. Faith was not a faculty with 'a constitutive power': it was merely the 'power of recognition'.[6] The creation of systems, parties, schemes and projects are all alike futile or otiose, because that is the work of building not digging. The only proper function for a Christian teacher was—to teach.

This was Maurice's most insistent, and perhaps also most profound, message as a theologian. As far as his immediate disciples were concerned, it seemed to them his bane. It sentenced their master to inaction and impotence, when he might have used his genius to advance the cause of Christian Socialism and co-operative workshops. Maurice's answer was, it seemed, to let things be. If the law of society seemed to be competition, this was a failure to recognize that God had proclaimed that law to be co-operation. But if the law had been proclaimed, it was futile to set up organizations to realize what God had already established. It took J. M. Ludlow some time to realize why he and F. D. Maurice were continually at cross-purposes; and when he did so, he fastened upon the metaphor of 'digging', from which he believed all Maurice's errors sprang:

I don't believe you, thank God, I won't and I can't [he wrote]. . . . Surely the whole work of Christianity is building and not digging, just as digging was the work, the only true work, of the heathen philosopher, until the corner-stone be laid. . . . Dear friend, will you allow me to say that I have felt that this *was* one of your temptations? I have endeavoured to study you very closely for the last year, both in yourself and thro' your books . . . and it does seem to me that you are liable to be carried away by Platonistic dreams about an Order, and a Kingdom, and a Beauty, self-realised in their own eternity, and which so put to shame all earthly counter-parts that it becomes labour lost to attempt anything like an earthly realisation of them, and all one has to do is to show them, were it only in glimpses, to others by tearing away the cobwebs of human systems that conceal them. I do not think this is Christianity.[7]

Appendix D

Ludlow may have found Maurice difficult to understand; but as a description of Christian Platonism, his letter is incomparable. 'Where is wisdom found, and where is the place of understanding?' poses the Book of Job. The answer, says Maurice, lies in the book of Proverbs, 'Man is to dig for it as for hid treasure'.[8] It is the answer of all Platonists who must seek, even as Coleridge did, that 'other World that *now* is, and ever has been, tho' undreamt of by the Many'.[9]

APPENDIX E

Platonism and the Concept of 'Clerisy'

It is one of the conventional truisms of political theory that Plato was an élitist and Aristotle 'the first Whig'. Without exploring the weakness of this statement as a generalization, we might, however, admit that Plato in the *Republic* certainly taught that it was not given to the multitude of men to be philosophical and that power ought to reside with the few who had the ability to discern the truth. Conversely, Aristotle criticized Plato's concept of the Guardians and taught, both in the *Politics* and the *Ethics*, that the many have a sort of corporate wisdom, based on the dubious principle that the good elements tend to outweigh the bad, and that an ethical or aesthetic judgment by the multitude is therefore more likely to be right than wrong.[1]

Coleridge was attracted to esoteric writings and had the deepest respect for mystics, visionaries, gnostics and the like, even though he might make public profession of his distrust of fanaticism.[2] He was as fully acquainted with the concept of the *disciplina arcani* as it appears in the writings of the Neoplatonists as ever Blake was. He believed, however, that in all men there was the potential to employ the imaginative power and that reason itself was a universal attribute. The point is made in *The Friend*. '*Reason itself* is the same in all men,' he wrote, 'yet the means of exercising it, and the materials (i.e. the facts and ideas) on which it is exercised, being possessed in very different degrees by different persons, the *practical Result* is, of course, equally different.'[3] But the fact that the potential was there meant that there was every hope and purpose in appealing to this rational power. Coleridge had a compulsive desire to educate and to expound. As soon as he encountered a new subject, or a new train of thought, his first inclination was to write a book about it. It was a duty for the educated to act, as it were, as monitors over those who were ignorant or blind.

In this sense, there had to be an élite in society. This was a fact of life; but a fact which involved the recognition of a duty and a responsibility.

> Alas! dear Sir! [Coleridge wrote to T. G. Street in March 1817] What is Mankind but *the Few* in all ages? Take them away, and how long, think you, would the rest differ from the Negroes or New Zealanders?[4]

All progress and amelioration in the history of the world, he wrote in *The Friend*, have come about through the efforts of 'the successive Few in every age . . . I appeal to the Histories of the Jewish, the Grecian, and the Roman Republic, to the Records of the Christian Church, to the History of Europe from the Treaty of Westphalia (1648). What do they contain but accounts of noble structures raised by the wisdom of the few, and gradually undermined by the ignorance and profligacy of the many?'[5] The most that one could hope for was that the wisdom of the few should elevate the many not to a state of understanding the truth, but at least of recognizing that they should regulate their lives by it. 'It is the privilege of the few to possess an idea', Coleridge wrote in his essay on the *Constitution of Church and State*: 'of the generalities of men, it might be more truly affirmed that they are possessed by it.'[6]

There can be no doubt that Coleridge found his teaching in Plato. He despised popularizers as much as Plato despised sophists. A purveyor of wisdom who was not a lover of wisdom was a menace to society, and for exactly the reason that Plato gave in the *Republic*. Plato had allegorized the sophist as the 'keeper of some high and powerful creature' who made a study of its moods and always sought to flatter its vanity, so that 'good or bad, right or wrong' became terms fitted 'to the fancies of the great beast', and accordingly such a keeper would 'call what it enjoys good and what vexes it bad'.[7] In like manner, Coleridge defined a popular work as one 'which gives back to the people their own errors and prejudices, and flatters the many by creating them, under the title of THE PUBLIC, into a supreme and inappellable tribunal of intellectual excellence'.[8] It was the duty of the élite, as it was the duty of Plato's guardians, to protect the many from the blandishments of the type of leader or teacher whom they, in their unwisdom, thought most likely to give them what they wrongly supposed to be their needs.

Coleridge found the simple *rationale* for this: which was to become, we may note, one of the leading ideas of the Victorian age, on which so much of its vigour and greatness was based, supplying its dynamism and didacticism, its assurance and its arrogance. Knowledge is Power. Arnold taught it to his pupils; Kipling lectured on it; Gladstone took it as the only foundation for a true aristocracy; the British Empire, it could be argued, was built on it. A disciplined mind, Coleridge observed, 'acquires not only a facility of recurring frequently to the sources and fountain heads of truth . . . ; but this process becomes a want, an habitual desideratum of his nature, the cause the more pleasurable because he progressively finds himself more and more amply remunerated both by the power which he acquired over others in anticipating the conclusion of minds formed in the same school as his own, and the delusions of others which he overlooks as one placed on an elevation in the centre of a labyrinth of paths not only sees his own future direction but can safely prophesy the entanglements and wanderings of the groundlings at every turn and in the whole detail of error'.[9] Knowledge is power. It is 'the axiom of education'.[10]

If knowledge is power, power belongs to those who know—or at least a particular sort of power should be recognized as belonging to those in a position to know. This was how Coleridge saw the Clerisy. In every social unit there should be some germ of civilization, some 'nucleus' round which 'the capabilities of the place may crystallize and brighten'.[11] He traced this historically as existing within the parish in the person of the clergyman; and when he came, in the *Constitution of Church and State* to express this function within the terms of the estates of the realm, he broadened the concept into that of the 'Clerisy . . . or national Church' comprehending 'the learned of all denominations, the sages and professors of the law and jurisprudence, of medicine and physiology, of music, of military and civil architecture, of the physical sciences . . . ; in short, all the so-called liberal arts and sciences, the possession and application of which constitute the civilization of a country, as well as the theological'.[12] Its function was to provide the element of cultivation, where the other two orders were to stand for the principles of permanence and progression. But cultivation there must be if society were to be healthy rather than corrupt and its people 'polished' rather than 'varnished'. The Clerisy, in short, stood for 'the harmonious development of those qualities and faculties that characterize our humanity. We must be men in order to be citizens.'[13]

They are not guardians, these *literati*, these sages of the professional classes. They are rather monitors. They articulate the conscience of a nation, for a society without a conscience becomes a mob. 'Multitudes never blush.'[14] Something of similar type may be seen again, in the guise of John Stuart Mill's leisured academics pointing the way to the legislators with cogent reasons and in Matthew Arnold's more attractive, because more urbane, seekers after culture disseminating the superior qualities of sweetness and light. They are both variations of 'clerisy', and both have Platonic assumptions even if they strive to avoid a too manifest contempt for representative institutions.

But this was not Newman's élitism. There are moments, indeed, when it seems so. The supercilious dismissal of John Bullism in 'Who's to Blame?' certainly has the tone—as David Delaura pointed out—of Plato's contemptuous disdain for the uninformed public-spiritedness of the Athenians.[15] He occasionally gave vent to gloomy prognostications on the advent of democracy.[16] There was also a fastidiousness and aloofness in Newman's temperament which so appealed to Matthew Arnold that he would cheerfully have handed over the monitorial capacity within the nation to those who combined such urbanity, percipience and charm. But Newman himself never wrote of a clerisy or showed any interest in Coleridge's writings on this theme.

The 'Holy Party' and
Brooke Foss Westcott

As far as the 'Holy Party' was concerned, the influence of T. H. Green stands out. It would not be accurate, however, to describe Green as a Platonist. He was certainly very critical of Aristotle, as was shown in his major review of Sir Alexander Grant's edition of the *Ethics*, although his own social philosophy (the notion that one serves God best by serving man) was very close to Aristotle's own.[1] On the other hand, *The Principles of Political Obligation*, as Melvin Richter has pointed out, was a philosophy belonging 'to the same logical family as those criticised by Professors Popper and Berlin',[2] and Green's concept of the divine power, dimly espied but in reality at work in every created thing ('the mind of man' being 'the only manifestation which can enjoy the consciousness of its perfect original'[3]) was very Wordsworthian and intensely Platonic. In actual fact, Green repudiated the concept of two rival traditions in Greek philosophy, and was happy to draw from both philosophers as he was prepared to criticize them when occasion arose.[4]

Melvin Richter has suggested four elements in Green's teaching which profoundly affected his Oxonian pupils and which were later manifested in the theology of those who were prepared to resist Green's scruples about commitment to any one of the Christian Churches. One of these—the rejection of materialistic values and the horror of hedonism—betokened an attitude of mind rather than a theological standpoint, but the other three were all related to a concept of the role of the Incarnation. Green's social philosophy— his belief that 'a Church unconnected with its effect upon the political justice and social welfare of its society cannot be said to be the bearer of the gospel taught by Jesus'[5]—found expression in the writings of Gore, Holland and Temple in their representation of the

Appendix F

Incarnation as the supreme example of the principle of involvement in the sufferings and passions of human society. Green's teaching that life is for action (the prime message of his *Lay Sermons*) was a more appealing challenge to young men than Maurice's more sober warnings on the futility of parties and organization, and was eagerly translated by Holland into a dynamic definition of faith. Whereas to Maurice, faith was merely recognition, Holland saw it as 'an active principle, a source of energy, a spring of movement; . . . It verifies itself only in actions: its reality can only be made evident through experience of its living work.'[6]

The final element of Green's teaching is more obviously related to Logos theology. Green emphasized that the Christian message was a progressive revelation which could be seen at work in every manifestation of the genius of man, a direct anticipation of the theological elaboration of the same idea in the contributions of Aubrey More and J. R. Illingworth to *Lux Mundi*. Furthermore, Green pictured the world itself as 'the realisation of a spiritual principle',[7] whereby the divine purpose was gradually fulfilled, a concept which could easily be translated into the terms of evolutionary science and immanentist theology.

All these ideas could be found in Westcott, who owed nothing to T. H. Green, and little of a direct nature to F. D. Maurice, whose theology his own teaching so closely resembled.[8] In view of the unquestionable fact that both Gore and Holland were taught by Westcott at a very impressionable stage of their lives, it might be that their incarnationalism was derived more directly from him than from Green at Oxford. There is evidence to support this. Gore was a schoolboy at Harrow at the time when Westcott was still on the staff there, and although he did not meet Westcott frequently, he was deeply impressed by Westcott's sermon on 'The Disciplined Life' preached in the Harrow Chapel in 1868—so impressed, in fact, that when he was called upon to preach the University sermon at Oxford in 1894, he chose to speak on exactly the same text—'Look carefully how ye walk . . . because the days are evil'.[9] It is significant also that Westcott's cherished scheme to found a 'Coenobium', which he was prosecuting vigorously at the time that Gore was at Harrow, appears again as a proposal for inculcating the patristic ideal of communal living in Gore's pamphlet on the *Social Doctrine of the Sermon on the Mount*, where the grounds for such an experiment are presented in precisely the same terms that Westcott had used some thirty years earlier.[10].

It is sometimes forgotten, too, that Scott Holland studied for ordination under Westcott in July 1872. Holland had already been through his period of most intense discipleship to T. H. Green. When he came to Peterborough it was to find this teaching confirmed.

> He is a perfect teacher [Holland wrote]: we return from our lessons chanting rapturous litanies of Praise and Gratitude. Altogether I feel as if I were really making something of a start for theological reading: and I have acquired a new sense of what knowledge may be from Westcott.[11]

Westcott took him to the heart of St John's Gospel. 'He speaks of St. John's Gospel with a sort of hushed awe', Holland wrote to Fremantle; 'it is like Fra Angelico, he cannot venture to criticize a verse without a prayer'.[12] It is interesting that in the following year, Holland embarked on a serious study of Plato[13] and the fourth gospel which bore fruit in the most celebrated series of university lectures which he was to give as a Student of Christ Church, one course on the *Republic* and the other on St John. His pupils spoke of him as he had written of Westcott. 'To hear him lecture on Plato and on St. John was a memorable experience. . . . Plato and St John, between them, know all that we should ever know, and more, of God and man.' As it was said of Illingworth's lectures on St John, 'The Logos meant something then, meant everything—even the freshmen felt that it did.'[14]

Holland was back at Peterborough with Westcott in 1875 for a short period, contemplating some joint venture for extension lectures. In the following year, however, Westcott was engaged in a puzzling correspondence with E. W. Benson on the curious character of the Oxford mind. Cambridge men were Scotists, but Oxford men were Thomists as well (an interesting variation of Maurice's distinction), and Holland appeared to be deviating into an Augustinian theology. 'I am grieved to hear', Westcott wrote to Benson, 'that Holland follows Mylne in making sin the centre of his philosophy. Surely the true centre is "in the image of God made He him".'[15] Neither this letter, nor Benson's reply,[16] elucidate the circumstance of this alleged deviation, which must unfortunately remain an enigma. It does not detract, however, from the evidence which strongly points to Westcott having exercised an enduring influence over Holland's interpretation of St John and the doctrine of the Incarnation.

Apart from this, there appears to have been little cross-fertilization between the Oxford incarnationalists and the Cambridge 'trio' of Westcott, Lightfoot and Hort during the closing decades of the nineteenth century. Westcott would meet Holland and Gore in their common endeavours within the Christian Social Union, but the contributors to *Lux Mundi* failed to remark the closeness of their interpretation of the Incarnation to Westcott's teaching, and Westcott himself took so little interest in *Lux Mundi* that, as he told Benson in March 1890, he 'purposely refrained from reading' it, presumably on the same grounds as his reluctance to read Maurice —he might 'endanger his own originality'.[17] Westcott, then, worked on alone—even as he had arrived at his understanding of Plato and the Gospel of St John alone.

The crucial years for Westcott's own development had been his last years at Harrow and his short period as Canon of Peterborough. During this time he contributed the articles to the *Contemporary Review* on Plato, Aeschylus, Euripides, Origen and Dionysius the Areopagite, in which the basis of his Platonic theology was laid. In all these writers he found a common quest—the explanation of their understanding that 'the whole visible world appears as a progressive revelation of the One source of life'.[18] The pre-Christian writers wrote as prophets of the Logos; the others were Christians whose insight had been deepened by their study of Plato. Was there anyone in his own time who had found the words to express the meaning of their vision? Westcott believed that there was. It was not Coleridge, whom Westcott did not greatly admire;[19] it was not Maurice, fellow-worker though he might be; it was not Green, whose works Westcott scarcely knew. It was not a theologian or a philosopher at all; but a poet—Robert Browning.

Here—and here alone—Westcott and the *Lux Mundi* group were in accord in recognizing the poet of the Incarnation. Westcott explained it all to the Browning Society at Cambridge. In the first place, Browning was a true poet in his faculty for perceiving 'the infinite in things'.[20] He could survey the squalid and the sordid, the mean and the vile and not be discountenanced. 'He has brought back for us from his universal survey a conviction of hope.' However

miserable or brutish his subject, Browning 'finds a spiritual power
in him, answering to a spiritual power without him, which restores
assurance as to the destiny of creation'.[21] This aspect of Browning's
poetry, Westcott developed in his essay on 'The Relation of
Christianity to Art'. 'Christian Art is the interpretation of beauty in
life under the light of the Incarnation', he wrote. 'The ministry of
the beautiful in every shape, in sound, in form, in colour, is claimed
for God through man.'[22] So in *Fra Lippo Lippi* Browning tells us:

> This world's no blot for us
> Nor blank: it means intensely, and means good:
> To find its meaning is my meat and drink.[23]

The principle that lay behind this was the universal power of love.

> We're made so that we love,
> First when we see them painted, things we've passed
> perhaps a hundred times nor cared to see; . . .
> . . . Art was given for that.
> God uses us to help each other so,
> Lending our minds out.[24]

Browning was, in a sense, his own Pippa—the child, blessed with
just such intuitive vision as the earlier Romantics had ascribed to
childhood, who is so unworldly and guileless that she fails to notice
the ugliness of the scenes and characters that she meets in her passing,
but sees only the good and beautiful, so that she awakens a sense of
guilt and shame in those whom she meets, enabling them to see, for a
moment at least, their true selves. The reliance upon emotion and
instinct may be a long way indeed from Plato's concept of the
apprehension of higher truths, but it is very near to what Blake,
Coleridge, Wordsworth, Shelley and Newman had at different
times, and in different ways, perceived. It is near, too, to what
F. D. Maurice had meant when he told Edward Strachey that all
children were born Platonists. In Browning it is expressed as a firm
rejection of intellectualism. As Mr E. D. H. Johnson has put it:

In Browning's world, the prophets and artists, the lovers and
doers of great deeds are never primarily remarkable for intellectual prowess. Their supremacy is the result of a genius for experiencing life intuitively. They possess a phenomenal capacity for

passionate emotion, combined with a child-like reliance on instinct. . . . Whether it be Fra Lippi, or Rabbi Ben Ezra, or David in *Saul*, or the Grammarian, or Childe Roland, Browning's heroes are always children of their intuition.[25]

Secondly, Browning perceived life as a unity. It may not always seem so. This is because we do not see its 'many-sided completeness'; or because what we can do must necessarily seem incomplete compared to the perfection of eternity. 'On the earth the broken arcs; in the heaven a perfect round.'[26] Striving there must be. As it is put in *The Statue and the Bust*:

> Let a man contend to the uttermost
> For his life's set prize, be it what it will.

or

> And the sin I impute to each frustrate ghost
> Is, the unlit lamp and the ungirt loin.

And it is not in vain. Westcott explains the challenge thus: 'the poet teaches us that life now must be treated as a whole; that learning comes through suffering; that every failure felt to be failure points to final achievement; that the visible present is but one scene in an illimitable growth'.[27] And the life to come, or the eternal order, reflect the unity and the achievement. That is why we go on attempting the impossible.

> Ah, but a man's reach should exceed his grasp,
> Or what's a heaven for?[28]

Hope, unity, love, the spiritual principle at work in the world—this sums up the incarnationalism of the late nineteenth century. Scott Holland was as susceptible to this poetry as Westcott. He read a paper to the Browning Society in 1884 on 'The Flight of the Duchess';[29] and lamented to a young musician who had composed a song cycle from some of Browning's verses—'You set him to music. I set him to poor, flat, homely prose' (surely the most inappropriate adjectives ever applied to Holland's idiosyncratic style).[30] But the man who was to pay deepest homage to Browning was William Temple. All Temple's poets were Platonists—Shelley, first; then Coleridge (through filial respect, perhaps); then Spenser; then Browning—'the greatest product of the nineteenth century'.[31] As

Iremonger has written, 'there was a completeness in Browning which he found nowhere else', and the reason was that Browning had penetrated to the deepest truths of Christianity. 'To Browning the climax of history, the crown of philosophy, and the consummation of poetry, is unquestionably the Incarnation.'[32]

And with William Temple the incarnationalism of the late nineteenth century was taken into the twentieth; and with it, too, the Platonic tradition as it had been represented in English Romantic thought and theology. He was himself to see its power wane, as later generations found it increasingly difficult to read the essential goodness of man out of the carnage of total war or to hear the message of hope amidst cries of despair. Nevertheless the Platonic tradition remained the foundation of Temple's own philosophy and theology as he expounded it in *Mens Creatrix* and *Christus Veritas*; and it was in the first of these that he paid his tribute to those who had taught him where to seek the truth.

> It is said of Bishop Westcott [he wrote] that he held in especial veneration St John, Origen, and Browning. I do not in any way claim comparison with the great scholar and seer if I say that the first name and the third, with Plato's in place of Origen's, would designate the master influences upon my own thought.[33]

If Westcott had been permitted to speak for himself, Plato's name would have been there too.

Was Matthew Arnold
a Platonist?

Was Matthew Arnold a Platonist? Any attempt to give a definite
answer—such as the recent essay by Walter Hipple, arguing Arnold's
Platonism through his use of dialectic, notably the tension between
contrasting forces[1]—founders on the rocks of Arnold's cheerful and
disrespectful eclecticism. More than that: it fails to perceive the
essentially 'mediatorial' role which Arnold adopted as a critic. As
David Delaura has seen, the fundamental tension within Arnold
himself was to mediate between the teaching of his father and that
of John Henry Newman, leading him to a position 'at once liberal
and conservative, poetic and rationalistic'.[2] So in the relationship
between reason and faith (on the few occasions that Arnold allowed
himself to venture into epistemology), 'he steers a course', as Lionel
Trilling has put it, 'both by compass and by stars: reason, but not
the cold and formal reason that makes the mind a machine; faith,
but not the escape from earth-binding facts. "The main element of
the modern spirit's life", he says "is neither the senses and the understanding, nor the heart and imagination: it is the imaginative
reason".'[3] As soon as one succeeds in labelling Matthew Arnold, he
shows the other face. This is why descriptions of him, if they are
anywhere near the truth, have to be couched in paradox. He was,
as Chesterton put it, 'a fanatic of moderation'.[4] Apparently bland
and confident, he was a man, not so unlike Arthur Clough, very
near to despair; a prodigious reader and a lifelong eclectic, he was
sure of only one thing about the position that he must adopt—'I
have always sought to stand by myself'.[5]

Matthew Arnold was not a philosopher and not interested in the
sort of questions that philosophers raise. He disliked metaphysics
and had little patience with theology. The only philosopher of whom
he made more than passing mention was Spinoza, and this—one

suspects—was because Spinoza provided him with a stick with which to belabour 'negative' thinkers and 'weak triflers' of the stamp of Bishop Colenso. Also, as William Robbins has pointed out, Spinoza was both positive and vivifying, perhaps the only philosopher of both poetry and life, thus effecting the synthesis of imagination and conduct which Arnold himself tried to express in the enigmatic phrase 'Poetry is a criticism of life'.[6]

Arnold attacked *a priori* thinking, quoting Newton's *hypotheses non fingo*;[7] he praised Butler for his down-to-earth qualities,[8] and accused Plato of sophisticating Socrates[9] so that he became the founder of an esoteric and 'unprofitable' tradition.[10] Time and time again, he employed the law of experience as a test of truth. He admires Goethe, he wrote in a letter to his mother, because of his 'thorough sincerity—writing about nothing that he had not experienced'.[11] At the climax of *Literature and Dogma*, he explains that the best proof of his understanding of Christianity is to 'try it and see'.[12] In his *Discourses in America*, he poses the question, 'Have poetry and eloquence the power of calling out the emotions?' He answers: 'The appeal is to experience. Experience shows that for the vast majority of men, for mankind in general, they have the power.'[13]

All this is thoroughly Aristotelian. Whenever Arnold wrote of Aristotle (even when with a touch of irony in *Culture and Anarchy*, he recalls the over-weighted Aristotelian training of his time at Oxford),[14] he always treated him with respect. He employed the canon of the *Poetics* in criticizing the Romantic poets,[15] and even applied it—falsely, as Professor Culler has suggested[16]—in rejecting his own *Empedocles on Etna* from his collected poems. According to M. T. Herrick, Matthew Arnold became 'the staunchest Aristotelian poet-critic in his century'.[17] Now and again he will betray his Aristotelianism with an argument in syllogistic form;[18] his mediatorial, balancing spirit has a greater affinity to the Aristotelian doctrine of the mean than to Coleridge's concept of the reconciliation of opposites;[19] and it could be convincingly argued that his whole theory of the *Zeit-geist*, the idea, for instance, that perfection in culture is 'not a having and a resting, but a growing and a becoming',[20] is essentially teleological and therefore Aristotelian rather than Platonic.

With all this evidence in favour of Arnold's Aristotelianism, it would seem a futile exercise to suggest that there was anything of the

Platonist in him at all. But so there was. It comes out most clearly in his essay on Joubert.

> Joubert was all his life a passionate lover of Plato; I hope other lovers of Plato will forgive me for saying that their adored object has never been more truly described than he is here:—
> 'Plato shows us nothing, but he brings brightness with him; he puts light into our eyes, and fills us with a clearness by which all objects afterwards become illuminated. He teaches us nothing; but he prepares us, fashions us, and makes us ready to know all.'[21]

Now this in itself would not entitle us to suggest that Arnold was a Platonist. The tone, and the phrase 'adored object' is patronizing, and seems the more so when we meet the famous description by Joubert which Arnold was later to adopt—as the only good thing he could find to say—in his treatment of Shelley. 'Plato loses himself in the void . . . ; but one sees the play of his wings, one hears the rustle. . . . It is good to breathe his air, but not to live upon him.'[22] But the words originated from a lover of Plato, and Arnold's efforts to bring the names of Joubert before the English public were inspired by his conviction that in Joubert he had found a kindred spirit. As D. G. James rightly said, Arnold's curious predilection for little-known continentals like Senancour, Maurice de Guerin and Joubert was not just perversity: 'he had a way of nosing out people like himself'.[23]

Like himself; or at least like one part of Matthew Arnold. He craved for time to think; he wished also that his generation could find time to think. Poets and thinkers, pathetic, unsuccessful people, perhaps, who 'lost themselves in the void', who chose to be thinkers rather than doers, who cultivated good taste rather than commercial advancement, always attracted him—provided, of course, that they lived up to his somewhat exacting standards of good conduct. Shelley and Coleridge put themselves beyond the pale because of their failure to practise what they preached. Byron might have done likewise, but for his redeeming feature of aristocratic grace (to Arnold, conduct for the aristocracy might be allowed to be somewhat less than three-fourths of their lives, one cannot help feeling).[24] Ineffectiveness by the world's standards might be the price one had to pay for having style. This is why he praised Joubert; and why he was drawn to Plato. He wrote, in a letter to his mother, in 1863:

'Plato . . . could not in his day have been a man of action, and so one may say, perhaps, that no single man is or can be perfect. But certainly Plato would have been less perfect than he was had he entered the stock politics of Athens at his day.'[25]

The perfect man would have within him the Hebraic and Hellenistic elements nicely balanced. So, too, the perfect state. The trouble with England was that it had an overbalance of the Hebraic element, the result of the Protestant Reformation and the pernicious influence of the dissenting sects. America was even worse. If the condition of England presented a dismal spectacle of 'an upper class materialised, a middle class vulgarised, a lower class brutalised', America was 'just ourselves, with the Barbarians quite left out, and the Populace nearly'.[26] It was the quintessence of Philistinism. This means bad manners, bad taste, vulgarity.

> What people in whom the sense for beauty and fitness was quick could have invented, or could tolerate, the hideous names ending in *ville*, the Briggsvilles, Higginsvilles, Jacksonvilles, rife from Maine to Florida. . . . The mere nomenclature of the country acts upon a cultivated person like the incessant pricking of pins.[27]

It had all come about through 'the glorification of the "average man"' who was almost a religion in the United States. A glance at an American newspaper is enough to condemn the country from the start. 'It is often said that every nation has the government it deserves. What is much more certain is that every nation has the newspapers it deserves.'[28]

When Plato attacked the Athenians of his day, he did so in the spirit of Arnold attacking his own country or the United States. At least this is how Arnold himself saw it. And where Plato annoyed the Athenians by citing the lessons that could be learned from Sparta (of all places!), Arnold rubbed vinegar into the wounds of his countrymen by extolling the superiority of culture and manners in France. In fact one may go further. Plato was not only concerned with instilling a love of wisdom and beauty into his countryman (as Arnold was); above all, he strove to inculcate a love of the good, for the three were inextricably involved. Arnold realized this too. The core of Plato's teaching was that 'conduct is three-fourths of life';[29] the lover of wisdom must be the lover of good. The good writer is the good man. The intellectual and ethical virtues cannot be separated.

Appendix G

Arnold's Plato was the Plato of the *Republic*. He had no time for the purely metaphysical dialogues; although he had read the *Phaedrus* and the *Symposium* he rarely quoted from them, and when he did he chose the passages not about Platonic love, but about the instinct for good in all men.[30] The *Republic*, however, is the text for Arnold's élitism—his central teaching on the remnant who stand over against the Barbarians, the Philistines and the Populace for the virtues of 'sweetness and light'. When he condemned the popular notion of 'Doing as one likes' in *Culture and Anarchy*, he had in mind Book VIII of the *Republic*; he was fascinated by the allegory of the Great Beast;[31] he used imagery suggestive of the allegory of the Cave;[32] he pictured the remnant as Plato's philosopher sheltering under a wall as the storm raged about him.[33] For all Arnold's protestations of liberalism,[34] he believed in a strong state and in such an ordering of society that the cultivated few could make their opinions felt, for the remnant was the 'Holy Seed' of Isaiah, the 'chosen few'.[35] He contradicts Aristotle's doctrine of verification in the *Discourses in America*. The passion for equality was a bane—failure to recognize the necessary truth of that 'hard doctrine of the unsoundness of the majority'.[36] It is true that Arnold was not always logical here. If he could, he would have had it both ways. In his admiration for De Tocqueville, he recognized the futility of resisting democracy, and explained his teaching as the best way to prepare for it. But he was harsher than Mill on the toleration of stupid, minority opinions and far more ready to invoke the authority of the state within the sphere of education.[37]

One final word must be said of Arnold's élitism. Derived as it was from Plato, it was strengthened by his enduring regard for the richness of insight displayed by Newman. It was not only that Newman epitomized for Arnold that urbanity and gracefulness of touch which was the essence of 'sweetness and light'; it was also that Newman had perceived the cardinal truth that 'many are called but few chosen', and had been led (through his reading of the Alexandrian Platonists) to the realization that the divine mode of instruction was in accordance with the doctrine of economy. Arnold could not accept Newman's predestinarian connotations of his teaching, but his own study of solitary sages such as Senancour and Joubert convinced him that those who at any time might possess 'a privileged insight into truth' must be few.[38] The duty of the few was to attack philistinism wherever it was manifested, even as Newman had done; insofar as 'sweetness and light' could be taught, it might be inculcated in just such a University atmosphere as Newman had described in the *Idea*;[39] and if the ignorant multitude were to be infused with this higher sense of taste and style, then the wisdom of the few—and most particularly the appreciation of right conduct—would have to be translated by some reflection of the mode of teaching of Christ himself, by adaptation according to the needs and state of growth of those who were being instructed.[40]

Whatever, then, Arnold derived from Plato's *Republic*, he translated into a mental picture of a particular man (Newman) in a particular University (Oxford) at a particular time of rampant Philistinism and Barbarianism within the country at large. It is not, therefore, surprising that Oxford men should feel that while Arnold was inveighing against ignorance and blindness on a national scale, he was also saying something very particular to them.

Notes and References

INTRODUCTION *pp. 1–7*

1. Lionel Trilling, *Matthew Arnold* (1963 edn.), 256.
2. K. Coburn, introduction to S. T. Coleridge, *Philosophical Lectures* (1949), 54; N. Fruman, *Coleridge, The Damaged Archangel* (1971), 114–15.
3. Charles Lamb, *Essays of Elia* (Cambridge, 1921), 36.
4. S. T. Coleridge, *Specimens of the Table Talk*, ed. H. N. Coleridge (3rd edn. 1851), 2 July 1830, 100–1.
5. *Ibid.*, 100–1.
6. Basil Willey, *The English Moralists* (1964), 54.
7. J. A. K. Thomson, introduction to *The Ethics of Aristotle* (1953), 13.
8. Aristotle, *Nicomachean Ethics*, Book VI.
9. *Ibid.*, Book II, c. 7.
10. *Republic*, VI. 494.
11. Aristotle, *The Politics*, III, c. 15, 1286 a.
12. R. F. Brinkley (editor), *Coleridge on the Seventeenth Century* (Duke University, 1955), 366.
13. J. Morley, *Critical Miscellanies* (1886), I. 308.

Chapter One: PLATO AND THE ROMANTICS *pp. 8–24*

1. F. Maurice, *The Life of Frederick Denison Maurice* (1884), I. 206–7.
2. R. M. Ogilvie, *Latin and Greek. A History of the Influence of the Classsics on English Life from 1600 to 1918* (1964), 45–6, 50.
3. J. A. Notopoulos, *The Platonism of Shelley. A Study of Platonism and the Poetic Mind* (Durham, N. Carolina, 1949), 3–4.
4. J. E. Baker, 'Our new Hellenic Renaissance' in J. E. Baker (editor), *The Reinterpretation of Victorian Literature* (Princeton, 1950), 214.
5. Kathleen Raine and G. M. Harper (editors), *Thomas Taylor the Platonist. Selected Writings* (1969), 123.
6. R. D. Gray, *Goethe the Alchemist. A Study of Alchemical Symbolism in Goethe's Literary and Scientific Works* (Cambridge, 1952), 250–1.
7. Joseph Barrell, *Shelley and the Thought of his Time* (New Haven, 1947), 96.
8. J. A. Notopoulos, *op. cit.*, 52.
9. F. W. Stokoe, *German Influences in the English Romantic Period 1788–1818* (Cambridge, 1926), vi.
10. *Ibid.*, 89, 114.
11. S. T. Coleridge, *Biographia Literaria*, ed. J. Shawcross (1907), I, 99. See a discussion of this in A. O. Lovejoy, 'Coleridge and Kant's Two Worlds' in *Journal of English Literary History*, Vol. 7, no. 4 (1940), esp. 362.
12. *Biog. Lit.*, xli.

Notes and References

13. E. D. Hirsch, *Wordsworth and Schelling. A Typological Study of Romanticism* (New Haven, 1960), 4.

14. *Biog. Lit.*, I. 107. See also the discussion of this point in J. Isaacs, 'Coleridge's Critical Terminology' in *Essays and Studies*, XXI (1936), 97–9.

15. *Philosophical Lectures*, 54; *Lay Sermons*, ed. D. Coleridge (3rd edn. 1852), 124–5.

16. *Table Talk*, 100–1.

17. G. M. Harper, *The Neoplatonism of William Blake* (N. Carolina, 1961), 264.

18. R. F. Brinkley, *op. cit.*, 103.

19. *Philosophical Lectures*, 194.

20. John Beer, *Coleridge the Visionary* (1970 edn.), 60, 65.

21. John Livingston Lowes, *The Road to Xanadu. A Study in the ways of the Imagination* (1964 edn.), 223.

22. T. L. Peacock, *Nightmare Abbey* (1891 edn.), 95–6.

23. W. J. B. Owen, *Wordsworth's Preface to Lyrical Ballads* (*Anglistica*, IX, Copenhagen, 1957), 124.

24. *Biog. Lit.*, I. 202.

25. *Ibid.*, I. 202. On this (difference in degree rather than in kind), see the useful discussion in Owen Barfield, *What Coleridge Thought* (1971), 77, 82.

26. M. H. Abrams, *The Mirror and the Lamp. Romantic Theory and the Critical Tradition* (New York, 1958), 180.

27. Neville Rogers, *Shelley at Work. A Critical Enquiry* (1967), 308–9.

28. Northrop Frye, *Fearful Symmetry. A Study of William Blake* (Princeton, 1947), 13.

29. G. M. Harper, *op. cit.*, 102.

30. *Ibid.*, 102–3.

31. *Ibid.*, 103.

32. *Ibid.*, 130.

33. William Walsh, *The Use of the Imagination. Educational Thought and the Literary Mind* (1960), 51.

34. *Prelude*, I. 351–5.

35. *Modern Painters* in *Works*, V. 380–1, quoted by Jerome H. Buckley, *The Triumph of Time* (Cambridge, Mass., 1967), 65.

36. *Statesman*, 269–271. Cf. the myth of the earth-born, alluded to by the Eleatic Stranger which appears in *Republic*, III. 414–15.

37. *Timaeus*, 43.

38. B. Jowett, *Dialogues of Plato* (1871), III. 256.

39. *Adonis*, lii. See Paul Shorey's discussion of the lineage of this conception via Milton and Dante to the Neoplatonists in *Platonism, Ancient and Modern* (California, 1938), 54–7.

40. S. T. Coleridge, *Notebooks*, edited K. Coburn (1957), I. no. 1561. Cf. entry no. 556; also *Collected Letters of S. T. Coleridge*, edited E. L. Griggs (Oxford, 1956–71), II. no. 634.

41. *Endymion*, I. 795–7.

42. E. D. Hirsch, *op. cit.*, 134.

43. G. W. F. Hegel, *Logic*, trans. W. Wallace (Oxford, 1892), 33–4.
44. *Collected Letters*, II. 709, no. 385.
45. *Philebus*, 58.
46. *Republic*, VI. 509–11.
47. *Symposium*, 210–11.
48. S. T. Coleridge, *The Friend*, edited Barbara E. Rooke (Princeton, 1969), I. 115.
49. A. E. Powell, *The Romantic Theory of Poetry* (1926), 96.
50. J. G. Davies, *The Theology of William Blake* (1948), 76.
51. J. H. Muirhead, *Coleridge as Philosopher* (1930), 113–14.
52. N. Frye, *op. cit.*, 14–15.
53. M. H. Abrams, *op. cit.*, 131.
54. Neville Rogers, *op. cit.*, 122.
55. *Ibid.*, 156–7.
56. *Collected Letters*, I. 349, no. 209.
57. J. G. Davies, *op. cit.*, 22; G. M. Harper, *op. cit.*, 98.
58. N. Frye, *op. cit.*, 15.
59. Milton O. Percival, *William Blake's Circle of Destiny* (New York, 1938), 50.
60. See H. S. Davies, 'Wordsworth and the Empirical Philosophers' in *The English Mind. Studies in the English Moralists*, edited H. S. Davies and G. Watson (Cambridge, 1964), 166–7.
61. *The Tables Turned*, 21–5.
62. N. Frye, *op. cit.*, 26.
63. *Auguries of Innocence*, 1–4.
64. S. T. Coleridge, *Aids to Reflection*, edited D. Coleridge (1854), 139. 'A grain of sand sufficing, and a whole universe at hand to echo the decision.' T. McFarland discusses the Swedenborgian origins of the idea in *Coleridge and the Pantheist Tradition* (Oxford, 1969), 129.
65. Poem in a letter to Butts, 2 October 1800: G. M. Harper, *op. cit.*, 229–30 N. Frye, *op. cit.*, 42.
66. J. B. Beer, *Blake's Humanism* (Manchester, 1968), 198–9.
67. 'The more decorous version appealing from Philip drunk to Philip sober' was:

> The Poet in his lone yet genial hour
> Gives to his eye a magnifying power;
> Or rather he emancipates his eyes
> From the black shapeless accidents of size—
> In unctuous cones of kindling coal,
> Or smoke upwreathing from the pipe's trim bowl,
>   His gifted ken can see
>   Phantoms of sublimity.

J. Livingston Lowes, *op. cit.*, 371–2. The cosmological side of this— expressed in very Plotinian language—may be seen in *The Æolian Harp*, 44–8 (*Complete Poetical Works of S. T. Coleridge*, edited E. H. Coleridge (1895), I. 102).

Notes and References

68. Paul Tillich, *Perspectives on Nineteenth and Twentieth Century Protestant Theology* (1967), 96–7.

Chapter Two: THE VISION OF THE CHILD *pp. 25–40*

1. Lionel Trilling, *The Liberal Imagination. Essays on Literature and Society* (1951), 131. This view is challenged by T. M. Raysor in 'The Theme of Immortality and Natural Piety in Wordsworth's Immortality Ode' in *Publications of the Modern Languages Association* (PMLA), LXIX (1954), 862–3.
2. C. M. Bowra, *The Romantic Imagination* (1961 edn.), 86. The fullest account of the circumstances of the writing of the Ode may be found in *The Journals of Dorothy Wordsworth*, ed. W. Knight (1938), 103–4; M. Moorman, *William Wordsworth. A Biography* (Oxford, 1957), I. 553–4. On Hartley Coleridge's connection with the Ode, see Herbert Hartmann, 'The Intimations of Wordsworth's *Ode*' in *Review of English Studies*, VI. no. 22 (1930), 130.
3. *Wordsworth's Poetical Works*, ed. E. de Selincourt (Oxford, 1940–7), IV, 463–4.
4. See the controversy in *Modern Language Notes*, XXXIII (Baltimore, 1918), 246–8 (contribution by E. A. White) and 497–8 (by Lane Cooper).
5. The Thomas Taylor translations of *Cratylus, Phaedo, Parmenides*, and *Timaeus*, J. A. Notopoulos, *op. cit.*, 164.
6. Argued strongly in J. D. Rea, 'Coleridge's Intimations of Immortality from Proclus' in *Modern Philology*, Vol. 26 (1928–9), 201–2. See also J. Livingston Lowes, *op. cit.*, 211 and *Collected Letters*, I. 260–1, no. 156.
7. Walter Pater, *Plato and Platonism* (1910), 73–4.
8. R. F. Brinkley, *op. cit.*, 617–19.
9. J. S. Mill, *Dissertations and Discussions, Political, Philosophical and Historical* (1875), III. 350–1.
10. Alec King, *Wordsworth and the Artist's Vision* (1966), 106.
11. *Phaedrus*, 249.
12. *Phaedo*, 72–3. 'Cebes added: Your favourite doctrine, Socrates, that knowledge is simply recollection, if true, also necessarily implies a previous time in which we learned that which we now recollect. But this would be impossible unless our soul was in some place before existing in the human form; here there is another argument of the soul's immortality.'
13. *Meno*, 81.
14. *Euthydemus*, 306.
15. *Meno*, 96–7.
16. *Phaedo*, 77.
17. *Gorgias*, 464. Cf. Callicles scorning full-grown men 'lisping as . . . a child', or children misconceiving their own roles by 'carefully articulating' their words, *ibid.*, 485.
18. *Sophist*, 234–5.
19. I owe these two references to Dr Elizabeth Stopp, who was present at

this particular lecture at Cambridge. As opposed to Schlegel and Schleiermacher, she writes, 'I think that something much closer to Coleridge's view, and Blake's, comes in Novalis' *Die Lehrlinge zu Sais*, the beginning of a novel, where the child appears as the prophet and teacher, having all the answers to the riddle of the universe. This idea also pervades the whole work of the artist, Ph. Otto Runge—who has close affinities with Blake. It is also a feature of some of Clemens Brentano's *Märchen*, especially the *Gockelmärchen* in its final version. . . . Novalis also has some striking "Fragmente" about "the child".'

20. Hegel, *Logic*, 131–2.
21. *Ibid.*, 55; cf. p. 254 where the same argument is made.
22. R. R. Niebuhr, *Schleiermacher on Christ and Religion* (1965), 40. This is not, however, associated in his writings with the Platonic doctrine of *anamnesis*. In his discussion of this in his introductions to the *Meno* and the *Phaedo*, Schleiermacher is mainly concerned with the proof of immortality of the soul, and the assistance which the different forms of the discussion provide in dating the dialogues. F. Schleiermacher, *Introductions to the Dialogues of Plato*, trans. W. Dobson (1836), 301–3.
23. R. R. Niebuhr, *op. cit.*, 50.
24. *Table Talk*, 9 August 1832.
25. Discussed in J. Robert Barth, *Coleridge and Christian Doctrine* (Cambridge, Mass., 1969), 173–4.
26. Peter Coveney, *The Image of Childhood. The Individual and Society* (1967 edn.), 43.
27. *Prelude*, V. 398.
28. H. Crabb Robinson, *Diary, Reminiscences, and Correspondence*, ed. T. Sadler (1869), II. 303.
29. *Aids*, 148.
30. *Table Talk*, 105. See also *Collected Letters*, IV. 860; *The Friend*, I. 499–500.
31. *Collected Letters*, I. 354–5, no. 210. Cf. no. 209 and *On Logic and Learning*, edited A. D. Snyder (New Haven, 1929), 127.
32. *Collected Letters*, I. 347.
33. *Ibid.*, I. 349.
34. J. H. Newman, *Apologia pro Vita sua* (1913 edn.), 105–6.
35. J. H. Newman, *Historical Sketches* (1873), II. 387–8.
36. *Notebooks*, II. no. 2329.
37. F. D. Maurice, *Moral and Metaphysical Philosophy* (1882), I. 194.
38. Such a distinction is certainly suggested in *Biog. Lit.*, I. 20, 30.
39. *Prelude*, V. 364–7. Cf. 483–7 for Wordsworth's admiration for the *Arabian Nights*.
40. *Songs of Experience*, 'The Schoolboy', 11, 23–4. See the comments on this in D. G. Gillham, *Blake's Contrary States. The Songs of Innocence and of Experience as Dramatic Poems* (Cambridge, 1966), 212.
41. H. N. Fairchild, *Religious Trends in English Poetry* (New York, 1949), III. 73.
42. C. M. Bowra, *op. cit.*, 29.

Notes and References

43. G. M. Harper, *op. cit.*, 70.
44. *Ibid.*, 66. Cf. p. 61. 'in my Brain are studies and Chambers fill'd with books and pictures of old, which I wrote and painted in ages of Eternity before my mortal life.'
45. *Ibid.*, 63–4.
46. J. A. Notopoulos, *op. cit.*, 36.
47. *Ibid.*, 36–7.
48. Morton D. Paley, *Energy and the Imagination. A Study of the Development of Blake's Thought* (Oxford, 1970), 36 and n. 2.
49. Deborah Dorfman, *Blake in the Nineteenth Century. His Reputation as Poet from Gilchrist to Yeats* (New Haven, 1969), 17 n. 12.
50. *Collected Letters*, IV. no. 1116.
51. *Prelude*, II. 334–7.
52. *Poetical Works*, I. 154, and note, referring to a letter to Poole, 1 Nov. 1796. But compare *Collected Letters*, I. 261 no. 156 where Coleridge quotes the poem with a note 'alluding to Plato's doc. of Pre-existence (S.T.C.).' See G. M. Harper, 'Gems of Purest Ray' in E. Blunden and E. L. Griggs (editors), *Coleridge. Studies by Several Hands* (1934), 141. There is, however, an earlier reference in *Religious Musings* (1794–6), lines 34–6.
53. *Destiny of Nations*, 18–23. Cf. also *Dejection. An Ode*, 84–6.
54. *The Friend*, I. 510. Coleridge read the poem to Von Humboldt.
55. R. F. Brinkley, *op. cit.*, 618–19.
56. *Biog. Lit.*, II. 111–12.
57. *Ibid.*, II. 120–1. Cf. *The Friend*, I. 195, where he admits that children have the faculty of reason, 'but in them the faculty is not adequately developed'.
58. *Notebooks*, II. no. 2332. Cf. no. 2546, where Coleridge writes of 'the dim Awaking of a forgotten or hidden Truth of my inner Nature', also referring to symbol in the sense which he uses it in *The Destiny of Nations*.
59. *Collected Letters*, I. 352–3, no. 210.
60. *The Friend*, II. 8.
61. *Collected Letters*, II. 1014, no. 525.
62. *Ibid.*, II. 802, no. 440.
63. H. Crabb Robinson, *op. cit.*, I. 341–2.
64. See *Collected Letters*, II. 673, no. 379.
65. *Ibid.*, II. 1024, no. 530.
66. *Ibid.*, II. 1014, no. 525.
67. Walter Bagehot, *Literary Studies* (1879), I. 41.
68. *Ibid.*, I.42.
69. A. E. Powell, *op. cit.*, 138.
70. *Ibid.*, 138.
71. Edwin Muir, *An Autobiography* (1954), 33, quoted in J. B. Beer, *Blake's Humanism*, 204.

Notes and References

Chapter Three: OPPOSITES AND CONTRARIES *pp. 41–56*

1. F. Maurice, *Life of F. D. Maurice*, I. 54–6.
2. *Collected Letters*, IV. 775, no. 1077.
3. *The Friend*, I. 94 n.
4. *Theaetetus*, 156–7.
5. *Ibid.*, 161.
6. *Euthydemus*, 285–6.
7. *Theaetetus*, 189.
8. *Protagoras*, 331.
9. *Philebus*, 13.
10. *Protagoras*, 340.
11. *Phaedo*, 70–1.
12. *Ibid.*, 103–5.
13. S. T. Coleridge, *On the Constitution of the Church and State*, edited H. N. Coleridge (1839), 126–7.
14. A. D. Snyder, 'Coleridge on Giordano Bruno' in *Modern Language Notes*, XLII (1927), 435. Owen Barfield argues convincingly that much of what Coleridge thought he discovered in Bruno came in fact from Boehme. O. Barfield, *op. cit.*, 186–7, 263.
15. *Symposium*, 189–193.
16. The chief sources for this fascinating subject are Kathleen Raine, *Blake and Tradition* (1969), Desirée Hirst, *Hidden Riches. Traditional Symbolism from the Renaissance to Blake* (1964), and Frances A. Yates, *Giordano Bruno and the Hermetic Tradition* (1964). A detailed account of androgynous symbolism in *Kubla Khan* may be found in John Beer, *Coleridge the Visionary*, 207–13.
17. M. O. Percival, *op. cit.*, 13. Cf. also the figure of Ulro as a hermaphrodite in *ibid.*, 70.
18. *Ibid.*, 91–3.
19. Quoted in *ibid.*, 93.
20. J. B. Beer, *op. cit.*, 118.
21. R. D. Gray, *op. cit.*, 34.
22. Details from *ibid.*, 17–18, 34–5.
23. *Table Talk*, 162. 13 March 1832.
24. *Collected Letters*, II. 713–4, no. 390.
25. R. D. Gray, *op. cit.*, 102–3. Cf. Boehme on this in D. Hirst, *op. cit.*, 90–91.
26. R. F. Brinkley, *op. cit.*, 397–8. Discussed, with references to seventeenth-century researches on magnetism, in O. Barfield, *op. cit.*, 35–7, 138–139.
27. *Ibid.*, 454 (from the marginalia to Browne, *Vulgar Errors*).
28. See especially, *The Friend*, I. 478–9.
29. H. Crabb Robinson, *op. cit.*, I. 165–6.
30. Hegel, *Logic*, 222. Cf. the discussion of this in the *Philosophy of Nature* in J. N. Findlay, *Hegel. A Re-examination* (1958), 270–1.
31. Hegel, *Logic*, 223.

Notes and References

32. I do not know the author, so cannot make the appropriate acknowledgement. I am grateful, however, to Dr R. D. Gray of Emmanuel College, Cambridge, for passing this on to me.
33. M. D. Paley, *op. cit.*, 69.
34. From the 'Argument' to *The Marriage of Heaven and Hell*. M. H. Abrams (*Mirror and the Lamp*, 216) describes this as 'a world-view which came remarkably close to that of German romantic philosophy', while acknowledging its source in the Neoplatonic esoteric tradition.
35. M. D. Paley, *op. cit.*, 12–13.
36. *Philebus*, 47.
37. Hegel, *Logic*, 149–151.
38. *Notebooks*, I. 1017.
39. *Ibid.*, II. 2329.
40. *Ibid.*, II. 2398n.
41. T. L. Peacock, *op. cit.*, 50.
42. Discussed in R. S. Franks, *The Work of Christ. A Historical Study of Christian Doctrine* (1962), 526.
43. K. Barth, *The Word of God and the Word of Man* (1928), 73, 209. My debt to Mr J. G. Davies (*op. cit.*, 138–9), who comments on these two quotations in his discussion of Blake's *coincidentia oppositorum*, must be recorded here.
44. F. D. Maurice, *Moral and Metaphysical Philosophy*, I. 143–4.
45. *Table Talk*, 59. 30 April 1830.
46. T. McFarland, *op. cit.*, 137–8.
47. W. Kaufmann, *Hegel. Reinterpretation, Texts and Commentary* (1966), 88. Cf. Hegel, *Logic*, 67.
48. See *Notebooks*, II. 2596. Cf. *Anima Poetae*, ed. E. H. Coleridge (1895) 147; *Biog. Lit.*, I. 170; *Collected Letters*, IV. 567, no. 966.
49. *Notebooks*, I. 1551.
50. S. T. Coleridge, *Lay Sermons*, edited D. Coleridge (1852), 92.
51. *Aids*, 55.
52. *Philosophical Lectures*, 178–9.
53. *Table Talk*, 199. 1 Sept. 1832. Cf. 227 (for Burke), 8 Apr. 1833.
54. *Ibid.*, 146–7, 12 Sept. 1831.
55. The most obviously Coleridgean passage on the polarity of truth in J. C. Hare may be found in J. C. Hare, *Charges* (1856), I. lxi, 93. Cf. also Duncan Forbes, *The Liberal Anglican Idea of History* (1950), 125.
56. J. S. Mill, *Dissertations*, I. 437.
57. *Ibid.*, I. 356. On the notion of 'half-thinkers' or—in Carlyle's phrase—'half-men', see the discussion in Edward Alexander, *Matthew Arnold and John Stuart Mill* (1965), 2–5.

Chapter Four: COLERIDGE AND NEWMAN *pp. 57–72*

1. F. Maurice, *op. cit.*, I. 182.
2. J. H. Newman, *Essays, Critical and Historical* (1872), I. 268.
3. J. D. Boulger, *Coleridge as Religious Thinker* (New Haven, 1961), 50.

Notes and References

4. J. H. Newman, *Lectures on the Prophetical Office of the Church* (1837).
5. The Anglican Church as a 'mean'—see George Herbert's poem which represents the Church of Rome as 'the painted lady on the hills' and the German Reformed Church as 'the undrest lady in the valley'. The Church of England was on the plain between them. 'But dearest Mother (what these miss)/The mean thy praise and glory is/And long may be.'
6. *Apologia*, 150.
7. *Ibid.*, 132.
8. J. H. Newman, *Lectures on Justification* (1838), 298.
9. *Ibid.*, 300.
10. J. D. Boulger, *op. cit.*, 50–3.
11. *Tracts for the Times*, no. 73, 53.
12. Graham Hough, 'Coleridge and the Victorians' in *The English Mind*, 187.
13. *Apologia*, 264.
14. J. H. Newman, *An Essay in aid of a Grammar of Assent* (1906 edn.), 499.
15. *Table Talk*, 269–70. 4 August 1833.
16. Owen Chadwick, *From Bossuet to Newman. The Idea of Doctrinal Development* (Cambridge, 1957), 186.
17. J. L. Altholz, *The Liberal Catholic Movement in England. The Rambler and its Contributors, 1848–1864* (1962), 166–8.
18. T. S. Bokenkotter, *Cardinal Newman as a Historian* (Louvain, 1959), 70.
19. J. H. Newman, *Letter . . . to the Duke of Norfolk* (1875), 104–5.
20. R. G. Collingwood, *The Idea of History* (Oxford, 1961 edn.), 274.
21. *Table Talk*, 232–4. 14 April 1833. Cf. O. Barfield, *op. cit.*, 161 where the point is made that to Coleridge all history was the history of thought.
22. J. S. Mill, *Dissertations*, I. 437–8.
23. *Ibid.*, I. 394.
24. Such a viewpoint is not expressed in Catholic thought until the Modernists apply a dynamic, evolutionary theory of revelation. Loisy expressed the absurdity of determining the nature of the Church from its original form when he wrote: 'The Church of today resembles, no more and no less, the community of the first disciples than an adult man resembles the infant which he was at first.' (A. R. Vidler, *Twentieth Century Defenders of the Faith* (1965), 43.) See also the discussion of Tyrrell's evolutionary concept of development in A. R. Vidler, *The Modernist Movement in the Roman Church* (Cambridge, 1934), 167.
25. See the point discussed in Sheldon Rothblatt, *The Revolution of the Dons, Cambridge and Society in Victorian England* (New York, 1968), 114.
26. J. H. Newman, *An Essay on the Development of Christian Doctrine* (1845), 39.
27. A. Dwight Culler, *The Imperial Intellect. A Study of Newman's Educational Ideal* (New Haven, 1955), 41.
28. *Ibid.*, 40.
29. G. M. Young, *Daylight and Champaign* (1948), 55.
30. J. H. Newman, *Loss and Gain. The Story of a Convert* (1903 edn.), 98.

Notes and References

31. The syllogism, basically, is: 'A university is a place for teaching universal knowledge' (J. H. Newman, *The Idea of a University* (1891 edn.), Preface, ix); 'Religious doctrine is knowledge' (*ibid.*, 42); *ergo*, a University is a place to teach religious doctrine, or 'University Teaching without Theology is simply unphilosophical'. (*Ibid.*, 42.)
32. *Ibid.*, 74–5.
33. *Ibid.*, 76.
34. J. H. Newman, 'Poetry, with reference to Aristotle's Poetics' in *Essays Critical and Historical*, I. 1–26; so critical was it that Blanco White 'good-humouredly only' described it as 'Platonic', 29.
35. *The Idea of a University*, 109–10.
36. *Ibid.*, 280.
37. *Ibid.*, 408.
38. *Essays Critical and Historical*, I. 287–8.
39. J. H. Newman, *Fifteen Sermons preached before the University of Oxford* (1918 edn.), 226–7.
40. *Grammar of Assent*, 415–8.
41. *Ibid.*, 414–5.
42. J. B. Mozley, *Lectures and other Theological Papers* (1883), 281.
43. *Ibid.*, 278.
44. *Grammar of Assent*, 353–7.
45. *Ibid.*, 361–71.
46. *Ibid.*, 362.
47. E.g. his very first University sermon, *University Sermons*, 7; and an interesting connection between this subject and discussions with Blanco White at Oriel, see D. Newsome, *The Parting of Friends* (1966), 87–9.
48. *Grammar of Assent*, 354.
49. *The Friend*, I. 524.
50. *Idea of a University*, 331–2. This idea is discussed briefly as an instance of Newman's psychological insight in W. Ward, *Last Lectures* (1918), 136–7.
51. Henry Tristram (editor), *John Henry Newman. Autobiographical Writings* (New York, 1957), 150.
52. *Table Talk*, 234. 14 April 1833.
53. *Aids*, 101. Cf. 140; *The Friend*, I. 513.
54. *Letters of S. T. Coleridge*, edited E. H. Coleridge (1895), I. cxxxviii. 427.
55. *Philosophical Lectures*, 174–5.
56. D. Emmett, 'Coleridge on the Growth of the Mind' in K. Coburn (editor), *Coleridge. A Collection of Critical Essays* (New Jersey, 1967), 168.
57. W. R. Inge, *Outspoken Essays*, 1st series (1920), 189.
58. *Apologia*, 105–6.
59. C. F. Harrold, 'Newman and the Alexandrian Platonists' in *Modern Philology*, xxxvii (1940), 281.
60. Thomas Acland came to this conclusion after reading the *Arians*, i.e. that Newman believed that the material world was 'a sacramental manifestation of the spiritual one in the best Coleridgean style'. Newman

was disturbed by this. H. Francis Davis, 'Was Newman a Disciple of Coleridge?' in *Dublin Review* (1945), 168.

61. J. H. Newman, *The Arians of the Fourth Century. Their Doctrine, Temper and Conduct* (1833), 83.

62. John Beer, 'Newman and the Romantic Sensibility' in *The English Mind*, 196-7. Father Ignatius Ryder, however, recollected Newman's admiration for the Immortality Ode: 'I do not think he ever took cordially to Wordsworth. That poet's didactic tone, his almost sacerdotal pretensions, offended him, and he was wearied by his excessive deliberations. But never shall I forget—I was a boy at the time, just recovering from an illness—his coming and reading to me the famous Ode "On the Intimations of Immortality". There was a passion and a pathos in his voice that made me feel that it was altogether the most beautiful thing I have ever heard.' (W. Ward, *Life of Newman*, 1912, II. 354. Cf. also, 336.) I am grateful to Dr John Beer for drawing my attention to these references.

63. G. M. Harper, *op. cit.*, 46-58.

64. *Ibid.*, 50.

65. G. M. Young, *op. cit.*, 57.

Chapter Five: PLATO AND INCARNATIONALISM *pp. 73-90*

1. Warren D. Anderson, *Matthew Arnold and the Classical Tradition* (Ann Arbor, 1965), 10-11.

2. Matthew Arnold, *Last Essays on Church and Religion* (1877), 62-4.

3. Goldwin Smith, *Reminiscences* (1910), 65.

4. D. C. Lathbury (editor), *Correspondence on Church and Religion of W. E. Gladstone* (1910), II 163-4.

5. *Ibid.*, II. 164.

6. Aristotle, *Nicomachaean Ethics*, I. IV. 5. See A. Grant, *The Ethics of Aristotle* (1874), I. 430 n.

7. *Philosophical Lectures*, 148.

8. F. D. Maurice, *Moral and Metaphysical Philosophy*, I. 188-90.

9. J. S. Mill, *Dissertations*, IV. 195.

10. *Ibid.*, III. 276.

11. *Ibid.*, III. 281.

12. J. S. Mill, *Four Dialogues of Plato*, ed. R. Borchardt (1946), 36-7.

13. *Ethics*, VI. 8. i.e. an adult quality as opposed to the Romantics' vision of the child. It is discussed in connection with Thomas Arnold by J. B. Mozley, who expresses the distinction thus: 'Young minds can evolve their own ideas and be philosophical, but they cannot have experience before they have acquired it.' J. B. Mozley, *Essays Historical and Theological* (1878), II. 65. On the equation of Aristotelianism with 'common sense', see also M. T. Herrick, *The Poetics of Aristotle in England* (New Haven, 1930), 141.

14. Walter Bagehot, *Literary Studies*, II. 65.

15. *The Oxford Quarterly Magazine*, I no. 1 (1825), 1-10.

16. On the role of William Sewell, see William Sewell, *Christian Morals* (1840), 44; William Tuckwell, *Reminiscences of Oxford* (1900), 234–5; Frederick Meyrick, *Memories of Life at Oxford and elsewhere* (1905), 112; Lionel James, *A Forgotten Genius. Sewell of St Columba's and Radley* (1945), 252–3. On Mark Pattison, see M. Pattison, *Essays*, ed. H. Nettleship (Oxford, 1889), I. 424.
17. G. R. G. Mure, 'Oxford and Philosophy' in *Philosophy*, XII (1937), 296.
18. E. Abbott and L. Campbell, *Life and Letters of Benjamin Jowett* (1897), I. 261.
19. A. M. M. Stedman, *Oxford: its social and intellectual life, with Remarks and Hints on Expenses, the Examinations, the Selection of Books etc.* (1878), 240.
20. A. M. M. Stedman, *Oxford: its Life and Schools* (1887), 251.
21. *Ibid.*, 253.
22. The 'Realists' v. the 'Idealists', superbly described and critically assessed in R. G. Collingwood, *An Autobiography* (1939) 15–20.
23. Ernest Barker, *Age and Youth* (1953), 319.
24. J. H. Newman, *The Idea of a University*, 144–5.
25. G. M. Young, *Today and Yesterday. Collected Essays and Addresses* (1948), 115. But compare Λ. E. Taylor, *Platonism and its Influence* (1925), 3, where a similar claim is made for Plato restoring civilisation to a world in turmoil.
26. R. Robson, 'Trinity College in the age of Peel' in R. Robson (editor), *Ideas and Institutions in Victorian Britain* (1967), 326 n. 2.
27. *Ibid.*, 326, n. 2.
28. *Ibid.*, 327.
29. *Republic*, 503 A. See also B. F. Westcott, *The Gospel according to St. John* (1894 edn.), xvii.
30. B. F. Westcott, *op. cit.*, xv.
31. C. Ackerman, *The Christian Element in Plato and the Platonic Philosophy*, trans. S. R. Asbury (1861), 20–21.
32. J. H. Newman, *The Arians of the Fourth Century*, 100–1.
33. B. M. G. Reardon, *From Coleridge to Gore. A Century of Religious Thought in Britain* (1971), 6, 14.
34. *Table Talk*, 94–5. 6 June 1830.
35. W. R. Inge, *The Platonic Tradition in English Religious Thought* (1926), 12–13.
36. B. F. Westcott, *Essays in the History of Religious Thought in the West* (1891), 246–7, 249.
37. *Philosophical Lectures*, 241.
38. B. F. Westcott, *Essays*, 238.
39. *Ibid.*, 345.
40. *Ibid.*, 2–6.
41. *On Logic and Learning*, 86–7.
42. A. M. M. Stedman, *Oxford: its Social and Intellectual Life*, 107.
43. G. R. G. Mure, *op. cit.*, 298–300.
44. J. E. C. Bodley, *Cardinal Manning, and other essays* (1912), 13.

45. Matthew Arnold, *Literature and Dogma* (1876), 132–7. As expressed by John Holloway, 'Arnold wishes to purge Christianity of what there is in it that is unprovable'. See John Holloway, *The Charted Mirror* (1960), 158.
46. For elaboration of this, see Lionel Trilling, *Matthew Arnold* (1902), 169–70, 173; Gertude Himmelfarb, *Victorian Minds. Essays on Nineteenth-Century Intellectuals* (1968), 156.
47. Edward Alexander, *op. cit.*, 174.
48. *Ibid.*, 174–5.
49. L. Gottfried, *Matthew Arnold and the Romantics* (1963), 46–7.
50. E. Alexander, *op. cit.*, 175–6.
51. Max Beerbohm, *Zuleika Dobson* (1952 edn.), 165.
52. Henry Scott Holland, *A Bundle of Memories* (1915), 312.
53. *Ibid.*, 63–4.

Appendix A: REASON AND IMAGINATION

1. O. Barfield, *op. cit.*, 96–7, 117. Memorably expressed in Basil Willey, *Nineteenth Century Studies: Coleridge to Matthew Arnold* (1964 edn.), 19–39.
2. See, for instance, T. McFarland, *op. cit.*, 35–7.
3. J. D. Boulger, *Coleridge as Religious Thinker* (New Haven 1961), 68–9.
4. T. McFarland, *op. cit.*, xxxiv–v.
5. *Aids*, 182–3n. Cf. Kant, *Critique of Pure Reason*, trans. N. Kemp Smith (1968), 69, for the same figure to illustrate *a priori* reasoning. See also for a very Kantian distinction between observation of a triangle and *a priori* understanding of its necessary and certain form, *Collected Letters*, II, 1198, no. 634. For Fancy being a part of Imagination, see *Table Talk*, 280, 20 August 1833; and for Understanding being an ingredient of Reason, see *The Friend*, I. 157; also I. A. Richards, *Coleridge on Imagination* (1934), 75.
6. *Anima Poetae*, 41–3; A. D. Snyder, *Coleridge on Logic and Learning* (New Haven, 1929), 12–13.
7. A. D. Snyder, *op. cit.*, 31.

Appendix B: ANTINOMIES, CONTRADICTIONS AND CONTRARIES

1. Kant, *Critique of Pure Reason*, 446.
2. *Ibid.*, 446.
3. See the good discussion of this in D. Emmet, *op. cit.*, 165–6. Antinomies are 'contradictory alternative views between which it is impossible to decide, because there is no evidence to which we can appeal to decide one way or the other'. Also Kant, *Inaugural Dissertation and Early Writings on Space*, trans. J. Handyside (Chicago, 1929), 80.
4. Discussed in J. S. Mill, *Dissertations*, IV. 208 f.
5. J. N. Findlay, *op. cit.*, 64.
6. Hegel, *Logic*, 100.
7. *Ibid.*, 119. Cf. 67.

8. W. Kaufmann, *op. cit.*, 193, 200, 212–13.
9. G. R. G. Mure, *An Introduction to Hegel* (Oxford, 1940), 141.
10. Discussed, with other references, in J. B. Beer, *Blake's Humanism*, 170.
11. See N. Frye, *op. cit.*, 180.
12. *Biog. Lit.*, I. 197.
13. *The Friend*, I. 160. He gives an example of an 'absolute contradiction'—a will acting without freewill—in *Aids*, 105.
14. A seeming inconsistency here is Coleridge's use of 'contrary' in *Notebooks*, 2839, where he writes of a proposition—'not a mere negative Impossibility but with the Reflection that it is made impossible by the actual presence of a positive, and sure heart-wasting CONTRARY.'
15. *Notebooks*, I. 2502.
16. *Biog. Lit.*, I. 197.
17. R. F. Brinkley, *op. cit.*, 349.
18. *Church and State*, 24–5n.
19. *Ibid.*, 38.
20. *Ibid.*, 126–7.

Appendix C: COLERIDGE'S 'TRICHOTOMOUS LOGIC'

1. Aristotle, *Nicomachaean Ethics*, II. 6.
2. *Ibid.*, II. 7.
3. Aristotle, *Politics*, IV. xi. 3.
4. *Aids*, 161, 166.
5. *Ibid.*, 303 n. Cf. also *Collected Letters*, II. 1097, no. 576. 'Reason perishes in extremes.'
6. *Church and State*, 102–3.
7. *The Friend*, I. 213.
8. *Lay Sermons*, 48–50.
9. *Ibid.*, 50–1.
10. *Table Talk*, 166, 4 April 1832. For other examples of this, see *Aids*, 104, *Notebooks*, II. 2920, *Collected Letters*, IV. 711, no. 1047.
11. J. H. Muirhead, *op. cit.*, 86.
12. O. Barfield, *op. cit.*, 187.
13. *Philosophical Lectures*, 323.
14. E. D. Hirsch, *op. cit.*, 30.
15. R. F. Brinkley, *op. cit.*, 118–19.
16. A diagram of the Pythagorean tetractys may be found in W. J. Bate, *Coleridge* (1968), 217.
17. A. H. Armstrong (editor), *The Cambridge History of Later Greek and Early Medieval Philosophy* (Cambridge, 1967), 299–300.
18. *Phaedo*, 102.
19. *Aids*, 276–7. See the long discussion of the 'equatorial point' in the very complex letter to C. A. Tulk in *Collected Letters*, IV. 767–76, no. 1077. Also *Table Talk*, 265, 3 July 1833. 'Imitation is the mesothesis of likeness and difference. The difference is as essential to it as the likeness; for without the difference, it would be a copy or fac-simile. But to

borrow a term from astronomy, it is a librating mesothesis: for it may verge more to likeness as in painting, or more to difference, as in sculpture.'

20. Very full definition in *Aids*, 132–6n.
21. *Literary Remains*, IV (1839), 429 n.
22. *Table Talk*, 172, 24 April 1832.
23. E.g. R. F. Brinkley, *op. cit.*, 120–1.
24. *Ibid.*, 121.
25. *Church and State*, 46.
26. *Ibid.*, 34.
27. A. D. Snyder, 'The Critical Principle of the Reconciliation of Opposites' in *Contributions to Rhetorical Theory* (Ann Arbor, 1918), 28, 37–54.
28. S. T. Coleridge, *Confessions of an Inquiring Spirit* (1956 edn.), 35.
29. *Aids*, 198–9. See the criticism of Aristotle's antithesis of nature to art (footnote on p. 199), which Coleridge interprets as a confounding of *natura naturata* with *natura naturans,* so that the idea of God becomes no more than a hypothesis—'which most grievous error it is the great and characteristic merit of Plato to have avoided and denounced'.
30. *Church and State*, 127.
31. *Confessions of an Inquiring Spirit*, 79.
32. *The Friend*, I. 104–5. Cf. *Table Talk*, 153–4, 3 December 1831.
33. J. R. Barth, *op. cit.*, 98.
34. *The Friend*, I. 521.
35. J. D. Boulger, *op. cit.*, 156, 158.
36. E.g. J. R. Barth, *op. cit.*, 110.
37. *Literary Remains*, I. 389–90.
38. T. McFarland, *op. cit.*, 220.
39. *Table Talk*, 44–5, 8 July 1827; cf. 73, 15 May 1830; J. R. Barth, *op. cit.*, 93–4.
40. *Literary Remains*, III. 3.
41. J. D. Boulger, *op. cit.*, 138.
42. J. R. Barth, *op. cit.*, 94.
43. Discussed in the light of the interpretation of Hegel in a book by J. D. Morell by J. H. Muirhead, *The Platonic Tradition in Anglo-Saxon Philosophy* (1931), 160.
44. In *Jerusalem*, 55. 15. See J. G. Davies, *op. cit.*, 51.

Appendix D: FURTHER ASPECTS OF F. D. MAURICE'S PLATONISM

1. R. H. Hutton, *Essays Theological and Literary* (1880), I. 3.
2. E.g. A. R. Vidler, *F. D. Maurice and Company* (1966), 247; H. G. Wood, *Frederick Denison Maurice* (Cambridge, 1950), 36–8.
3. Expressly acknowledged in F. Maurice, *op. cit.*, I. 43.
4. Argued convincingly in F. H. Maclain, 'Maurice as Moralist. The Ethical Teaching of Frederick Denison Maurice', Cambridge Ph.D. thesis, 1968, Chapter 3.
5. *Aids*, 256 n.

6. F. Maurice, *op. cit.*, I. 341.
7. Torben Christensen, *Origin and History of Christian Socialism 1848–54* (Aarhus, Denmark, 1962), 306.
8. F. D. Maurice, *Moral and Metaphysical Philosophy*, I. 5. Cf. xxi: 'Discovery and revelation are, it strikes me, more nearly synonymous words than any which we can find in our language. I may call that which is withdrawn a cover or a veil.'
9. Applied by Miss A. D. Snyder to Coleridge in *On Logic and Learning*, 2.

Appendix E: PLATONISM AND THE CONCEPT OF CLERISY

1. E.g. *Republic*, VI. 494 ('The multitude can never be philosophical'): *Politics*, III. XI. 2 (The many better than the best few).
2. *Aids*, 325–7.
3. *The Friend*, I. 159.
4. *Collected Letters*, IV. 714, no. 1048.
5. *The Friend*, I. 61–2. Cf. Appendix A, II. 52 and *Aids*, 186. 'How comes it that the philosophic mind should, in all ages, be the privilege of a few?'
6. *Church and State*, 12.
7. *Republic*, VI. 493.
8. *Aids*, 180 n.
9. *On Logic and Learning*, 181.
10. *Church and State*, 66.
11. *Biog. Lit.*, I. 155.
12. *Church and State*, 49.
13. *Ibid.*, 46.
14. *Ibid.*, 112. See the discussion of this in A. R. Vidler, *The Orb and the Cross. A Normative Study in the Relations of Church and State* (1945), 39.
15. David J. Delaura, 'Matthew Arnold and John Henry Newman. The "Oxford Sentiment" and the Religion of the Future' in University of Texas *Studies in Literature and Language*, VI. Supplement (1965), 602.
16. E.g. W. Ward, *Life of Newman*, II. 513. 'What a dreadful thing this democracy is! How I wish Gladstone had retired into private life.'

Appendix F: THE 'HOLY PARTY' AND BROOKE FOSS WESTCOTT

1. R. L. Nettleship, 'Memoir of T. H. Green' in *Works of Thomas Hill Green* (1886), III. lxxi. He draws attention especially to 'the principle that the higher or rational nature in man is that in which the impulse to knowledge and the impulse to society have their common root; that this is what makes him most truly man and most like God; and that to promote the growth of this nature is the highest service that he can render to his fellow-men'.
2. Melvin Richter, *The Politics of Conscience. T. H. Green and his Age* (1964), 224–5.
3. T. H. Green, 'The Influence of Civilisation on Genius' in *Works*, III. 11.

4. E.g. T. H. Green, 'The Philosophy of Aristotle' in *ibid*, III. 46.

5. M. Richter, *op. cit.*, 124.

6. *Lux Mundi. A Series of Studies in the Religion of the Incarnation*, edited C. Gore (1891), 7; M. Richter, *op. cit.*, 126.

7. M. Richter, *op. cit.*, 125.

8. A very controversial point, discussed in A. R. Vidler, *F. D. Maurice and Company*, 272–7; D. Newsome, *Bishop Westcott and the Platonic Tradition* (Cambridge, 1969), 14.

9. G. L. Prestige, *The Life of Charles Gore* (1935), 9–10; James Carpenter, *Gore. A Study in Liberal Catholic Thought* (1960), 25–6. See B. F. Westcott, *Disciplined Life. Three Addresses* (1886). For Gore's sermon, see C. Gore, *Buying up the Opportunity* (1895). The two are compared in my article, 'The Assault on Mammon. Charles Gore and J. N. Figgis' in *Journal of Ecclesiastical History*, XVII (1966), 238–9.

10. Charles Gore, *The Social Doctrine of the Sermon on the Mount* (1904), 18.

11. John Foster, 'Henry Scott Holland 1847–1914' (unpublished Ph.D. thesis in the University of Wales, 1970), 48.

12. S. Paget, *Henry Scott Holland. Memoir and Letters* (1921), 59.

13. S. Paget, *op. cit.*, 73. Holland refers to grinding through 'a lot of Zeller on Plato'.

14. *Ibid.*, 82.

15. A. Westcott, *Life of Brooke Foss Westcott* (1903), I. 433.

16. A. C. Benson, *Life of Edward White Benson* (1899), I. 395.

17. A. Westcott, *op. cit.*, II. 68. He had not read it by 1894 (*ibid.*, II. 226), and I am not sure that he ever did.

18. B. F. Westcott, *Essays*, 109.

19. A. Westcott, *op. cit.*, I. 111.

20. B. F. Westcott, *Essays*, 253.

21. *Ibid.*, 254.

22. *Ibid.*, 322–3.

23. *Ibid.*, Westcott quotes this also in a speech at Sedbergh in 1896 (*Christian Aspects of Life*, 1901, 381).

24. A great favourite with the incarnationalists. Westcott quotes it in *Essays*, 331, refers to it in *The Incarnation and Common Life* (1893), 144. See also Richard Brook in *Foundations*, ed. B. H. Streeter (1913), 64; William Temple, *Mens Creatrix* (1917), 123, 131.

25. E. D. H. Johnson, *The Alien Vision of Victorian Poetry* (Princeton, 1952), 92–3.

26. *Abt Vogler*, quoted in *The Incarnation and Common Life*, 144.

27. B. F. Westcott, *Essays*, 256.

28. *Andrea del Sarto*, quoted in *Essays*, 332.

29. S. Paget, *op. cit.*, 80.

30. John Foster, *op. cit.*, 162.

31. F. A. Iremonger, *William Temple. Life and Letters* (1948), 46.

32. *Ibid.*, 47.

33. William Temple, *Mens Creatrix*, vii.

149

Notes and References

Appendix G: WAS MATTHEW ARNOLD A PLATONIST?

1. Walter J. Hipple, 'Matthew Arnold, Dialectician' in *University of Toronto Quarterly*, XXXII (1962), 1–26. The argument is that Arnold's 'method of reasoning is Platonic', especially because of his delight in operating with pairs of contraries. This is doubtful. 'Sweetness and light', for instance, are hardly contraries (p. 9). The appearance of contraries arises much more from Arnold's 'mediatorial' stance than any attempt to translate Plato's dialectical method into modern terms.
2. David J. Delaura, *op. cit.*, 575.
3. Lionel Trilling, *Matthew Arnold*, 194.
4. Gertrude Himmelfarb, *op. cit.*, 156.
5. D. G. James, *Matthew Arnold and the Decline of English Romanticism* (Oxford, 1961), 106–7. Cf. T. S. Eliot, *Selected Essays* (1951), 441. 'Arnold Hellenizes and Hebraizes in turn.' This is another way of putting the paradox.
6. William Robbins, *The Ethical Idealism of Matthew Arnold* (1959), 64–5.
7. Matthew Arnold, *Literature and Dogma*, 181. Cf. *St Paul and Protestantism* (in *Matthew Arnold, Dissent and Dogma*, ed. R. H. Super, Ann Arbor, 1968), 33. 'St Paul begins with these facts, and has not yet . . . called upon them to prove anything but themselves.'
8. *Literature and Dogma*, 347. Cf. *Last Essays on Church and Religion*, 65, 178. Arnold is also critical of Butler in these essays—99, 101, 112, 140.
9. *Literature and Dogma*, 177.
10. Matthew Arnold, *Essays in Criticism* (1905 edn.), II. 312.
11. G. W. E. Russell (editor), *Letters of Matthew Arnold* (1901), I. 11.
12. *Literature and Dogma*, 345. Cf. also 212, 295. The interesting relationship between this passage and Coleridge's similar exhortation in *Aids to Reflection* is discussed in L. Gottfried, *op. cit.*, 173–5.
13. Matthew Arnold, *Discourses in America* (1902), 119–20.
14. Matthew Arnold, *Culture and Anarchy* (1896), 46.
15. D. G. James, *op. cit.*, 59–60.
16. A. Dwight Culler, *Imaginative Reason. The Poetry of Matthew Arnold* (New Haven, 1966), 201–2.
17. M. T. Herrick, *op. cit.*, 166.
18. E.g. *Essays in Criticism*, I. 50. 'Genius is mainly an affair of energy, and poetry is mainly an affair of genius; therefore, a nation whose spirit is characterised by energy may well be eminent in poetry.'
19. E. K. Brown, *Matthew Arnold. A Study in Conflict* (Chicago, 1966), 125–126.
20. *Culture and Anarchy*, 9. Cf. *St Paul and Protestantism*, 10. (God defined as 'that stream of tendency by which all things seek to fulfil the law of their being'. M. N. Feltes, 'Matthew Arnold and the Modern Spirit' in *University of Toronto Quarterly*, XXXIII (1962), 31–3, compares this dynamic definition with the more static and Platonic one in *Literature and Dogma*.
21. *Essays in Criticism*, I. 294.

Notes and References

22. *Ibid.*, I. 294. The reference to Shelley occurs twice in *ibid.*, II, 203–4, 252.
23. D. G. James, *op. cit.*, 24; 26.
24. L. Gottfried, *op. cit.*, 109.
25. *Letters*, I, 456, 13 June 1868.
26. 'A Word about America' in *Five Uncollected Essays of Matthew Arnold*, ed. K. Allott (Liverpool, 1953), 3, 6.
27. 'Civilisation in the United States' in *ibid.*, 54. Cf. his remarks on dull English names in *Essays in Criticism*, I. 23–4.
28. *Five Uncollected Essays*, 56–7.
29. Paul Shorey, *op. cit.*, 72; W. D. Anderson, *op. cit.*, 95–6; see especially *Discourses in America*, 30.
30. *Discourses*, 106. He refers to Diotima's speech in the *Symposium*, where Socrates is told that all men desire the good. Cf. Paul Shorey, *op. cit.*, 227. See also *Culture and Anarchy*, 99, for Arnold's dismissal of the doctrine of the immortality of the soul in the *Phaedo* as 'over-subtle and sterile'.
31. W. D. Anderson, *op. cit.*, 121–2.
32. *Five Uncollected Essays*, 36.
33. *Discourses*, 10.
34. See the essay on 'The Future of Liberalism' in *Irish Essays*, discussed in Edward Alexander, *op. cit.*, 233–44.
35. *Discourses*, 16.
36. *Ibid.*, 56. But cf. the exceedingly Aristotelian argument in *Mixed Essays* (1880), 18—'Democracy is a force in which the concert of a great number of men makes up for the weakness of each man taken by himself.'
37. The conclusion of E. Alexander, *op. cit.*, 233, 246. Cf. a less generous estimate in M. Cowling, *Mill and Liberalism* (Cambridge, 1963), 22, 34–5.
38. David J. Delaura, *op. cit.*, 592–3.
39. *Ibid.*, 602. See also David J. Delaura, 'Pater and Newman: The Road to the Nineties' in *Victorian Studies* (1966), 31–44 on the very similar notion in Pater.
40. *Ibid.*, 596–7.

Bibliography

Place of publication is only given when it is other than London.

Abbott, E. and L. Campbell, *The Life and Letters of Benjamin Jowett*, 2 vols., 1897.

Abrams, M. H., *The Mirror and the Lamp. Romantic Theory and the Critical Tradition*, New York, 1958.

Ackermann, C., *The Christian Element in Plato and the Platonic Philosophy*, trans., S. R. Asbury, 1861.

Alexander, Edward, *Matthew Arnold and John Stuart Mill*, 1965.

Altholz, J. L., *The Liberal Catholic Movement in England. The 'Rambler' and its Contributors 1848–1864*, 1962.

Anderson, Warren B., *Matthew Arnold and the Classical Tradition*, Ann Arbor, 1965.

Aristotle, *Nicomachaean Ethics*, edited Sir Alexander Grant, 2 vols., 1874.

—, *The Politics*, edited Sir Ernest Barker, Oxford, 1948.

Armstrong, A. H. (editor), *The Cambridge History of Late Greek and Early Medieval Philosophy*, Cambridge, 1967.

Arnold, Matthew, *Letters of Matthew Arnold 1848–88*, edited G. W. E. Russell, 2 vols. 1901.

—, *Culture and Anarchy, An Essay in Political and Social Criticism*, 1869.

—, *Discourses in America*, 1902.

—, *Essays in Criticism*, 1st and 2nd series, 1905.

—, *Five Uncollected Essays*, edited K. Allott, Liverpool, 1953.

—, *Last Essays on Church and Religion*, 1877.

—, *Literature and Dogma, An Essay towards a better appreciation of the Bible*, 1876.

—, *Mixed Essays*, 1880.

—, *St Paul and Protestantism*, in *Dissent and Dogma*, edited R. H. Super, Ann Arbor, 1968.

—, *The Study of Celtic Literature*, 1891.

Arnold, Thomas, 'An Essay on the Right Interpretation and Understanding of the Scriptures' in *Sermons*, II. 1878.

Augustine, Saint, *The City of God*, edited R. V. G. Tasker, 2 vols., 1945.

Babbitt, Irving, *The New Laokoon. An Essay on the Confusion of the Arts*, 1910.

Bagehot, Walter, *Literary Studies*, 2 vols., 1879.

Baker, Joseph E. (editor), *The Reinterpretation of Victorian Literature*, Princeton, 1950.

Ballard, A. W., 'F. D. Maurice. A Retrospect' in *Church Quarterly Review*, CXL, 1945.

Bambrough, Renford (editor), *Plato, Popper and Politics. Some Contributions to a Modern Controversy*, Cambridge, 1967.

Bibliography

Barfield, Owen, *What Coleridge Thought*, 1971.

Barker, Ernest, *Age and Youth*, 1953.

Barrell, Joseph, *Shelley and the Thought of his Time. A Study in the History of Ideas*, New Haven, 1947.

Barth, Karl, *From Rousseau to Ritschl*, 1959.

—, *The Word of God and the Word of Man*, 1928.

Barth, J. Robert, *Coleridge and Christian Doctrine*, Cambridge, Mass., 1969.

Bate, W. J., *Coleridge*, 1968.

Beer, John B., *Blake's Humanism*, Manchester, 1968.

—, *Coleridge the Visionary*, 1962.

—, 'Newman and the Romantic Sensibility' in H. S. Davies and G. Watson (editors), *The English Mind, Studies in the English Moralists presented to Basil Willey*, Cambridge, 1964.

Beerbohm, Max, *Zuleika Dobson, or an Oxford Love Story*, 1952.

Benson, A. C., *The Leaves of the Tree*, 1911.

—, *The Life of Edward White Benson*, 2 vols., 1899.

Blake, William, *Poetical Works*, edited J. Sampson, 1943.

Bodley, J. E. C., *Cardinal Manning, and other Essays*, 1912.

Bokenkotter, T. S., *Cardinal Newman as an Historian*, Louvain, 1959.

Boulger, James D., *Coleridge as Religious Thinker*, New Haven, 1961.

Bowra, C. M., *The Romantic Imagination*, 1961.

Bremond, H., *A Literary History of Religious Thought in France*, trans. K. L. Montgomery, I. *Devout Humanism*, 1928.

Brilioth, Y., *The Anglican Revival. Studies in the Oxford Movement*, 1925.

Brinkley, R. F., (editor), *Coleridge on the Seventeenth Century*, Duke University, 1955.

Brooke, Stopford A., *The Life and Letters of F. W. Robertson*, 2 vols., 1873.

Brown, E. K., *Matthew Arnold, A Study in Conflict*, Chicago, 1966.

Buckley, Jerome Hamilton, *The Triumph of Time. A Study of the Victorian Concepts of Time, History, Progress and Decadence*, Cambridge, Mass. 1967.

Burn, W. L., *The Age of Equipoise. A Study of the Mid-Victorian Generation.* 1964.

Butler, Joseph, *Fifteen Sermons*, edited T. A. Roberts, 1970.

Cameron, J. M., 'Newman and the Empiricist Tradition' in J. Coulson and A. M. Allchin, *The Rediscovery of Newman. An Oxford Symposium*, 1967.

—, *The Night Battle. Essays*, 1962.

Carpenter, James, *Gore. A Study in Liberal Catholic Thought*, 1960.

Chadwick, Owen, *From Bossuet to Newman. The Idea of Doctrinal Development*, Cambridge, 1957.

Christensen, T., *The Origin and History of Christian Socialism, 1848–1854*, Aarhus, Denmark, 1962.

Church, R. W., *The Oxford Movement. Twelve Years, 1833–1845*, 1891.

Clarke, M. L., *Classical Education in Britain, 1500–1900*, Cambridge, 1959.

Coburn, K., *Inquiring Spirit. A New Presentation of Coleridge from his published and unpublished prose writings*, 1951.

—, see, Coleridge, S. T., *Notebooks* and *Philosophical Lectures*.

Bibliography

Coleridge, S. T., *Collected Letters of S. T. Coleridge*, edited E. L. Griggs, 4 vols., Oxford, 1956–9.
—, *Letters of Samuel Taylor Coleridge*, edited E. H. Coleridge, 2 vols., 1895.
—, *Unpublished Letters of S. T. Coleridge*, edited E. L. Griggs, 2 vols., 1932.
—, *The Notebooks of Samuel Taylor Coleridge*, edited K. Coburn, 1957.
—, *Aids to Reflection*, edited D. Coleridge, 1854.
—, *Anima Poetae*, edited E. H. Coleridge, 1895.
—, *Biographia Literaria*, edited J. Shawcross, 2 vols., 1907.
—, *Complete Poetical Works of S. T. Coleridge*, edited E. H. Coleridge, 2 vols., 1895.
—, *Confessions of an Inquiring Spirit*, edited H. St J. Hart, 1956.
—, *Lay Sermons*, edited D. Coleridge, 1852.
—, *Literary Remains*, edited H. N. Coleridge, 4 vols., 1836—9.
—, *On Logic and Learning*, edited A. D. Snyder, New Haven, 1929.
—, *On the Constitution of the Church and State, according to the Idea of Each*, edited H. N. Coleridge, 1839.
—, *Philosophical Lectures*, edited K. Coburn, 1949.
—, *Specimens of the Table Talk of S. T. Coleridge*, edited H. N. Coleridge, 1851.
—, *The Friend*, edited Barbara E. Rooke, 2 vols., Princeton, 1969.
—, *Treatise on Method*, edited A. D. Snyder, 1934.
Collingwood, R. G., *An Autobiography*, 1939.
—, *The Idea of History*, Oxford, 1961.
Cooper, Lane, 'Wordsworth's Knowledge of Plato' in *Modern Language Notes*, XXXIII, Baltimore, 1918.
Coveney, Peter, *The Image of Childhood. The Individual and Society. A Study of the Theme in English Literature*, 1967.
Cowling, Maurice, *Mill and Liberalism*, Cambridge, 1963.
Cox, G. V., *Recollections of Oxford*, 1868.
Culler, A. Dwight, *Imaginative Reason. The Poetry of Matthew Arnold*, New Haven, 1966.
—, *The Imperial Intellect. A Study of Newman's Educational Ideal*, New Haven, 1955.
Cupitt, D. 'Mansel's Theory of Regulative Truth' in *Journal of Theological Studies*, N. S. XVIII, Oxford, 1967.
Davies, H. Francis, 'Was Newman a Disciple of Coleridge?' in *Dublin Review*, no. 435, 1945.
Davies, H. S., 'Wordsworth and the Empirical Philosophers' in *The English Mind. Studies in the English Moralists presented to Basil Willey*, edited H. S. Davies and G. Watson, Cambridge, 1964.
Davies, J. G., *The Theology of William Blake*, 1948.
Delaura, David J., 'Matthew Arnold and John Henry Newman. The "Oxford Sentiment" and the Religion of the Future' in *Studies in Literature and Language*, VI, Supplement, University of Texas, 1965.
—, 'Pater and Newman. The Road to the Nineties' in *Victorian Studies*, 1966.
Dorfman, Deborah, *Blake in the Nineteenth Century. His Reputation as a Poet from Gilchrist to Yeats*, New Haven and London, 1969.
Eliot, T. S., *Selected Essays*, 1951.

Bibliography

Emmet, Dorothy M., 'Coleridge on the Growth of the Mind' in K. Coburn (editor), *Coleridge. A Collection of Critical Essays*, New Jersey, 1967.

Fairchild, H. N., *Religious Trends in English Poetry*, Vol. III, New York, 1949.

Feltes, M. N., 'Matthew Arnold and the Modern Spirit' in *University of Toronto Quarterly*, XXXII, 1962.

Findlay, J. N., *Hegel. A Re-examination*, 1958.

Fite, Warner, *The Platonic Legend*, New York, 1934.

Forbes, Duncan, *The Liberal Anglican Idea of History*, 1950.

Foster, John, 'Henry Scott Holland, 1847–1914', unpublished Ph.D. thesis in the University of Wales, 1970.

Foundations. A Statement of Christian Belief in Terms of Modern Thought, edited B. H. Streeter, 1913.

Franks, R. S., *The Work of Christ. A Historical Study of Christian Doctrine*, 1962.

Froude, J. A., *Short Studies on Great Subjects*, 4 vols., 1891.

Froude, R. H., *Remains*, edited J. H. Newman and J. Keble, 4 vols., 1838–9.

Fruman, N., *Coleridge. The Damaged Archangel*, 1971.

Gillham, D. G., *Blake's Contrary States. The 'Songs of Innocence and of Experience' as Dramatic Poems*, Cambridge, 1966.

Gladstone, W. E., *Studies subsidiary to the Works of Bishop Butler*, Oxford, 1896.

Gore, Charles, *Buying up the Opportunity*, 1895.

—, *Church and Society*, 1928.

—, *Dissertations on Subjects connected with the Incarnation*, 1895.

—, *The Social Doctrine of the Sermon on the Mount*, 1904.

—, see *Lux Mundi*.

Gottfried, Leon, *Matthew Arnold and the Romantics*, 1963.

Gray, R. D., *Goethe the Alchemist. A Study of Alchemical Symbolism in Goethe's Literary and Scientific Works*, Cambridge, 1952.

Green, T. H., *Works*, edited R. L. Nettleship, 3 vols., 1888.

Hamilton, William, *Discussions on Philosophy and Literature, Education and University Reform*, 1852.

Hare, Julius Charles, *Charges*, 1856.

—, *Guesses at Truth*, by Two Brothers, edited E. H. Plumptre, 1866.

—, *The Mission of the Comforter, and other Sermons*, 2 vols., 1846.

—, *The Victory of Faith and other Sermons*, Cambridge, 1840.

Harper, George Mills, 'Gems of Purest Ray' in E. Blunden and E. L. Griggs (editors), *Coleridge. Studies by Several Hands on the Hundredth Anniversary of his Death*, 1934.

—, *The Neo-Platonism of William Blake*, North Carolina, 1961.

—, see Raine, Kathleen.

Harrold, C. F., 'Newman and the Alexandrian Platonists' in *Modern Philology* XXXVII, 1940.

Hartman, Herbert, 'The Intimations of Wordsworth's Ode' in *The Review of English Studies*, VI, 1930.

Hegel, G. W. F., *Logic*, trans. W. Wallace, Oxford, 1892.

Herrick, M. T., *The Poetics of Aristotle in England*, New Haven, 1930.

Bibliography

Himmelfarb, Gertrude, *Victorian Minds, Essays on Nineteenth-Century Intellectuals*, 1968.

Hipple, Walter J., 'Matthew Arnold, Dialectician' in *University of Toronto Quarterly*, XXXII, 1962.

Hirsch, E. D., *Wordsworth and Schelling. A Typological Study of Romanticism*, New Haven, 1960.

Hirst, Desirée, *Hidden Riches. Traditional Symbolism from the Renaissance to Blake*, 1964.

Holland, Henry Scott, *A Bundle of Memories*, 1915.

Holloway, John, *The Chartered Mirror*, 1960.

—, *The Victorian Sage. Studies in Argument*, 1965.

Hort, F. J. A., 'Coleridge' in *Cambridge Essays, contributed by Members of the University*, 1856.

Hough, Graham, 'Coleridge and the Victorians' in H. S. Davies and G. Watson (editors), *The English Mind. Studies in the English Moralists presented to Basil Willey*, Cambridge, 1964.

Huizinga, Johann, *Erasmus of Rotterdam*, 1952.

Hutton, R. H., *Essays Theological and Literary*, 2 vols., 1880.

Inge, W. R., *Outspoken Essays*, 1st Series, 1920.

—, *The Platonic Tradition in English Religious Thought*, 1926.

Iremonger, F. A., *William Temple. Life and Letters*, 1948.

Isaacs, J., 'Coleridge's Critical Terminology' in *Essays and Studies by Members of the English Association*, XXI, 1936.

James, D. G., *Matthew Arnold and the Decline of English Romanticism*, Oxford, 1961.

—, *Scepticism and Poetry. An Essay on the Poetic Imagination*, 1937.

—, *The Romantic Comedy. An Essay on English Romanticism*, 1963.

James, Lionel, *A Forgotten Genius. Sewell of St Columba's and Radley*, 1945.

Johnson, E. D. H., *The Alien Vision of Victorian Poetry. Sources of the Poetic Imagination in Tennyson, Browning and Arnold*. Princeton, 1952.

Johnston, J. O., *Life and Letters of Henry Parry Liddon*, 1904,

Jowett, Benjamin, see Plato, *Dialogues*.

Kant, Immanuel, *Critique of Pure Reason*, trans. N. Kemp Smith, 1968.

—, *Inaugural Dissertation and Early Writings on Space*, trans. J. Handyside, Chicago, 1929.

Kaufmann, Walter, *Hegel. Reinterpretation, Texts and Commentary*, 1966.

Keats, John, *Poetical Works*, edited H. Buxton Forman, 1944.

Kent, John, *From Darwin to Blatchford. The Role of Darwinism in Christian Apologetic, 1875–1910*, 1966.

—, *The Age of Disunity*, 1966.

Kermode, Frank, *Romantic Image*, 1957.

King, Alec, *Wordsworth and the Artist's Vision. An Essay in Interpretation*, 1966.

Knowles, David, *The Evolution of Medieval Thought*, 1962.

Lathbury, D. C. (editor), *Correspondence on Church and Religion of W. E. Gladstone*, 2 vols., 1910.

Livingstone, R. W., *Greek Ideals and Modern Life*, Oxford, 1935.

Bibliography

Lovejoy, A. O., 'Coleridge and Kant's Two Worlds' in *Journal of English Literary History*, Vol. 7, no. 4., 1940.
—, 'Kant and the English Platonists' in *Essays Philosophical and Psychological in honour of William James*, 1908.
—, 'The Meaning of Romanticism for the Historian of Ideas' in *Journal of the History of Ideas*, II, 1941.
Lowes, J. Livingston, *The Road to Xanadu. A Study of the Ways of the Imagination*, 1964 edn.
Lux Mundi. A Series of Studies in the Religion of the Incarnation, edited C. Gore, 1891.
Mackenzie, Faith Compton, *William Cory, A Biography*, 1950.
Mackintosh, H. R., *Types of Modern Theology. Schleiermacher to Barth*, 1937.
Maclain, F. H., 'Maurice as Moralist. The Ethical Teaching of Frederick Denison Maurice', unpublished Ph.D. thesis in the University of Cambridge, 1968.
Mallet, C. E., *A History of the University of Oxford*, Vol. III, 1927.
Maurice, F., *The Life of Frederick Denison Maurice*, 2 vols., 1884.
Maurice, F. D., *Moral and Metaphysical Philosophy*, 2 vols., 1882.
McFarland, Thomas, *Coleridge and the Pantheist Tradition*, Oxford, 1969.
Meyrick, Frederic, *Memories of Life at Oxford, and elsewhere*, 1905.
Mill, John Stuart, *Dissertations and Discussions, Political, Philosophical and Historical*, 4 vols., 1875.
—, *Four Dialogues of Plato*, edited R. Borchardt, 1946.
Moorman, Mary, *William Wordsworth. A Biography*, 2 vols., Oxford, 1957.
Morley, John, *The Life of W. E. Gladstone*, 3 vols., 1903.
Mossner, E. C., *Bishop Butler and the Age of Reason*, New York, 1936.
Mozley, A., (editor), *The Letters and Correspondence of John Henry Newman*, 2 vols., 1891.
Mozley, J. B., *Essays, Historical and Theological*, 2 vols., 1878.
—, *Lectures and other Theological Papers*, 1883.
Mozley, J. K., *Some Tendencies in British Theology from the publication of Lux Mundi to the Present Day* 1951.
Muirhead, J. H., *Coleridge as Philosopher*, 1930.
—, *The Platonic Tradition in Anglo-Saxon Philosophy*, 1931.
Mure, G. R. G., *An Introduction to Hegel*, Oxford, 1940.
—, 'Oxford and Philosophy' in *Philosophy*, XII, 1937.
Nettleship, R. L., 'Memoir of T. H. Green' in *The Works of Thomas Hill Green*, Vol. III, 1886.
—, *Lectures on the Republic of Plato*, 1901.
Newman, J. H., *A Letter addressed to His Grace the Duke of Norfolk on the occasion of Mr Gladstone's recent expostulation*, 1875.
—, *An Essay in aid of a Grammar of Assent*, 1906.
—, *An Essay on the Development of Christian Doctrine*, 1845.
—, *Autobiographical Writings*, edited Henry Tristram, New York, 1957.
—, *Discussions and Arguments on various subjects* 1872.
—, *Essays Critical and Historical*, 2 vols., 1872.
—, *Fifteen Sermons preached before the University of Oxford*, 1918

Bibliography

Newman, J. H., *Historical Sketches*, 2 vols., 1873.
—, *Lectures on Justification*, 1838.
—, *Lectures on the Prophetical Office of the Church, viewed relatively to Romanism and Popular Protestantism*, 1837.
—, *Loss and Gain. The Story of a Convert*, 1903.
—, 'On the Rational Principle in Religion' in *Tracts for the Times*, III, no. 73, 1837.
—, *Parochial and Plain Sermons*, 8 vols., 1868.
—, *Sermons bearing on Subjects of the Day*, 1918.
—, *The Arians of the Fourth Century. Their Doctrine, Temper, and Conduct*, 1833.
—, *The Idea of a University*, 1891.
Newsome, David, *Bishop Westcott and the Platonic Tradition*, Cambridge, 1969.
—, *Godliness and Good Learning. Four Studies on a Victorian Idea*, 1961.
—, 'Newman and the Oxford Movement' in A. Symondson (editor), *The Victorian Crisis of Faith*, 1970.
—, 'The Assault on Mammon. Charles Gore and John Neville Figgis' in *Journal of Ecclesiastical History*, XLII, 1966.
—, *The Parting of Friends. A Study of the Wilberforces and Henry Manning*, 1966.
Niebuhr, R. R., *Schleiermacher on Christ and Religion*, 1965.
Notopoulos, James A., *The Platonism of Shelley. A Study of Platonism and the Poetic Mind*, Durham, N. Carolina, 1949.
Ogilvie, R. M., *Latin and Greek. A History of the Influence of the Classics on English Life from 1600 to 1918*, 1964.
Overton, J. H. and E. Wordsworth, *Christopher Wordsworth, Bishop of Lincoln*, 1890.
Oxford Quarterly Magazine, Vol. 1, no. 1, 1825.
Paget, Stephen, *Henry Scott Holland. Memoir and Letters*, 1921.
Paley, Norton D., *Energy and the Imagination. A study of the Development of Blake's Thought*, Oxford, 1971.
Parry, R. St. J., *Henry Jackson, O.M.*, Cambridge, 1926.
Pater, Walter, *Plato and Platonism*, 1910.
Pattison, Mark, *Essays*, edited H. Nettleship, 2 vols., Oxford, 1889.
Peacock, T. L., *Nightmare Abbey*, 1891 edn.
Percival, Milton O., *William Blake's Circle of Destiny*, New York, 1938.
Plato, *The Dialogues of Plato*, edited B. Jowett, 4 vols., 1871.
—, *The Republic*, edited F. M. Cornford, Oxford, 1941.
Popper, Karl R., *The Open Society and its Enemies*, 2 vols., 1957.
Powell, A. E., *The Romantic Theory of Poetry*, 1926.
Prestige, G. L., *The Life of Charles Gore*, 1935.
Preyer, Robert O., 'Coleridge's Historical Thought' in K. Coburn (editor), *Coleridge. A Collection of Critical Essays*, New Jersey, 1957.
Prickett, Stephen, *Coleridge and Wordsworth. The Poetry of Growth*, Cambridge, 1970.
Raine, Kathleen, *Blake and Tradition*, Princeton and London, 1969.
—, and G. M. Harper (editors), *Thomas Taylor the Platonist. Selected Writings*, 1969.

Bibliography

Ramsey, A. M., *From Gore to Temple. The Development of Anglican Theology between Lux Mundi and the Second World War*, 1960.

Raysor, T. M., 'The Themes of Immortality and Natural Piety in Wordsworth's Immortality Ode' in *Publications of the Modern Language Association of America* (PMLA), LXIX, 1954.

Rea, J. D., 'Coleridge's Intimations of Immortality from Proclus' in *Modern Philology* Vol. 26, 1928–9.

Reich, Klaus, 'Kant and Greek Ethics' in *Mind*, XLVII, 1939.

Richards, I. A., *Coleridge on Imagination*, 1934.

Richter, Melvin, *The Politics of Conscience. T. H. Green and his Age*, 1964.

Robbins, William, *The Ethical Idealism of Matthew Arnold. A Study of the Nature and Sources of his moral and religious ideas*, 1959.

Robinson, Henry Crabb, *Diary, Reminiscences, and Correspondence*, edited T. Sadler, 3 vols., 1869.

Rogers, Neville, *Shelley at Work. A Critical Enquiry*, Oxford, 1967.

Rothblatt, Sheldon, *The Revolution of the Dons, Cambridge and Society in Victorian England*, New York, 1968.

Rousseau, J. J., *Emile, ou l'Education*, 2 vols., Paris, 1912.

Sandars, C. R. *Coleridge and the Broad Church Movement*, Durham, N. Carolina, 1942.

Schleiermacher, F., *Introductions to the Dialogues of Plato*, trans. W. Dobson, 1896.

—, *On Religion, Speeches to its Cultural Despisers*, trans. J. Oman, 1893.

Sedgwick, Adam, *A Discourse on the Studies of the University*, New York, 1969.

Sewell, William, *Christian Morals*, 1840.

Shelley, P. B., *Poetical Works*, edited T. Richardson, 1943.

Shorey, Paul, *Platonism, Ancient and Modern*, California, 1938.

Sidgwick, Henry, *Memoir*, by A. S. and E. M. S., 1906.

—, *Miscellaneous Essays and Addresses*, 1904.

Smith, Goldwin, *Reminiscences*, 1910.

Snyder, Alice D. 'Coleridge on Giordano Bruno' in *Modern Language Notes*, XLII, 1927.

—, 'The Critical Principle of the Reconciliation of Opposites as employed by Coleridge' in *Contributions to Rhetorical Theory*, edited P. N. Scott, Ann Arbor, 1918.

—, see Coleridge, *On Logic and Learning* and *Treatise on Method*.

Soundings, Essays concerning Christian Understanding, edited A. R. Vidler, Cambridge, 1962.

Stanley, A. P., *The Life and Correspondence of Thomas Arnold*, 2 vols., 1858.

Stedman, A. M. M., *Oxford: its Social and Intellectual Life, with Remarks and Hints on Expenses, the Examinations, the Selection of Books, etc.*, 1878.

—, *Oxford: its Life and Schools*, 1887.

Stokoe, F. W., *German Influence in the English Romantic Period, 1788–1818*, Cambridge, 1926.

Talbot, E. S., *Memories of Early Life*, 1924.

Taylor, A. E., *Platonism and its Influence*, 1925.

Bibliography

Taylor, Thomas, *Selected Writings*, see under Raine, Kathleen and G. M. Harper.

Temple, William, *Mens Creatrix, An Essay*, 1917.

Tillich, Paul, *Perspectives on Nineteenth and Twentieth Century Protestant Theology*, 1967.

Trevor, Meriol, *Newman: Light in Winter*, 1962.

Trilling, Lionel, *Matthew Arnold*, 1939.

—, *The Liberal Imagination. Essays on Literature and Society*, 1951.

Tuckwell, William, *Reminiscences of Oxford*, 1900.

Vidler, A. R., *F. D. Maurice and Company*, 1966.

—, *The Modernist Movement in the Roman Church*, Cambridge, 1934.

—, *The Orb and the Cross. A Normative Study in the Relations of Church and State with Reference to Gladstone's Early Writings*, 1945.

—, *Twentieth-Century Defenders of the Faith*, 1965.

—, see *Soundings*.

Walsh, William, *The Use of Imagination. Educational Thought and the Literary Mind*, 1960.

Ward, Wilfred, *Last Lectures*, 1918.

—, *The Life of John Henry Cardinal Newman*, 2 vols., 1912.

Webb, C. C. J., *Religious Thought in the Oxford Movement*, 1928.

Wellek, René, *Immanuel Kant in England, 1793–1838*, Princeton, 1931.

Westcott, Arthur, *Life and Letters of Brooke Foss Westcott*, 2 vols., 1903.

Westcott, Brooke Foss, *An Introduction to the Study of the Gospels*, 1895.

—, *Christian Aspects of Life*, 1901.

—, *Christus Consummator. Some Aspects of the Work and Person of Christ in relation to Modern Thought*, 1886.

—, *Disciplined Life. Three Addresses*, 1886.

—, *Essays in the History of Religious Thought in the West*, 1891.

—, *Social Aspects of Christianity*, 1910.

—, *The Gospel according to Saint John*, 1894.

—, *The Gospel of the Resurrection*, 1902.

—, *The Incarnation and Common Life*, 1890.

Whately, Richard, *Elements of Logic*, 1829.

White, E. A., 'Wordsworth's knowledge of Plato' in *Modern Language Notes*, XXXIII, Baltimore, 1918.

Williams, Isaac, 'On Reserve in Communicating Religious Knowledge', Parts I and II, in *Tracts for the Times*, IV and V, nos. 80 and 87, 1838.

Williams, Raymond, *Culture and Society, 1780–1950*, 1953.

Willey, Basil, *Nineteenth-Century Studies*, 1949.

—, *The English Moralists*, 1964.

Winstanley, D. A., *Later Victorian Cambridge*, Cambridge, 1947.

Wood, H. G., *Frederick Denison Maurice*, Cambridge, 1950.

Wordsworth, Dorothy, *Journals*, edited W. Knight, 1938.

Wordsworth, William, *Poetical Works*, edited E. de Selincourt, 5 vols., Oxford, 1940–9.

—, *Preface to Lyrical Ballads*, edited W. J. B. Owen, in *Anglistica*, IX, Copenhagen, 1957.

Bibliography

Wordsworth, William, *The Prelude* (1805 edn.), edited E. de Selincourt, 1935.
Yates, Frances A., *Giordano Bruno and the Hermetic Tradition*, 1964.
Young, G. M., *Daylight and Champaign*, 1948.
—, *Today and Yesterday. Collected Essays and Addresses*, 1948.

Index

Abrams, M. H., 10
Acton, Lord, 61
Aeschylus, 122
Aids to Reflection (Coleridge), 23, 31, 52, 91–3, 100, 112
Alchemy, *coincidentia oppositorum* in, 47–8; its relation with Romanticism, 10
Alford, Henry, 78
Allen, John, 78
Anabaptism, and alchemy, 10
Analogy of Religion (Butler), 73–4
Anamnesis, 7, 20, 26–8, 34–40, 76, 90
Ancient Mariner (Coleridge), 14
Androgynes, and alchemy, 46–7; and Blake, 46–7; Plato on, 45–6
Anglicanism, as understood by Coleridge and Newman, 58–60. *See* Church of England
Antinomies, 44, 95–7
Antiquities of Athens (Stuart and Revett), 11
Apologia pro vita sua (Newman), 58, 61
Arabian Nights, 32–3, 37
Aristotelianism, alleged of St Paul, 51, and historical method, 61; at Oxford, 8, 57, 63–4, 72–8; compared to Platonism, 1–7, 13, 24; in T. H Green, 119; of Matthew Arnold, 85–7, 126–7; of Newman, 58, 61–9, 71–2
Aristotle, 90; and Plato, 4, 87, 115; Arnold on, 127, 130; definitions of contradictions in, 96; epistemology of, 4–7; his doctrine of the mean, 6, 52, 100; on collective wisdom, 7, 115; logical method of, 63–7, 74–6; Newman on, 65–6; on *phronesis*, 5, 67–9; works of, in Oxford 'Greats', 73–8
Arnold, Gottfried, 10
Arnold, Matthew, 17; and elitism, 118, 130–31; and Newman, 85–6, 126, 130–31; and Romantic Platonism at Oxford, 84–7; Aristotelian elements in, 55–7, 126–7; on Aristotle and Butler, 73; on Hebraism and Hellenism, 1, 129; Platonic elements in, 55–7, 126, 127–31

Arnold, Thomas, 73, 84, 117, 126
Athanasius, 70
Atonement, doctrine of, 80, 112
Augustine of Hippo, 81
Augustinianism, 30, 80–81, 107, 121
Aurora (Boehme), 9, 14, 45, 47

Bacon, Francis, 77
Bagehot, Walter, 38, 76
Balliol College, Oxford, 77, 87
Barfield, Owen, 102
Barker, Sir Ernest, 77
Barrell, Joseph, 11
Barth, J. Robert, 106
Barth, Karl, 53–4
Baxter, Richard, 52, 99, 102–3
Beer, John, 23
Beerbohm, Max, 87
Behmenism, 10. *See* Boehme, J.
Benson, E. W., 121–2
Bentham, Jeremy, 56, 62, 78
Berkeley, George, 12; and *coincidentia oppositorum*, 47; idealism of, 21
Berlin, Isaiah, 119
Biographia Literaria (Coleridge), 12–13, 15, 22, 37, 91, 98
Blake, Mrs William ('Kate'), 20
Blake, William, 15, 41, 90, 123; androgynous imagery in, 46–7; *coincidentia oppositorum* in, 51, 110; esoteric teaching of, 70–71, 115; his distrust of education, 31, 34–5; his influence on other Romantics, 36; his rejection of Locke, 14; influence of Boehme on, 11; on contraries and negations, 44, 51, 97–8; on vision, 20–24, 34–5; Platonism of, 15, 31, 35
Bodley, J. E. C., 84
Boehme, Jacob, 9, 12, 42, 45–7; and alchemy, 10; influence of, in England, 10–11
Boulger, J. D., 58–9, 106, 109
Bowra, C. M., 26
Bradley, F. H., 77
Brazen Serpent, The (Erskine), 112
Browning, Robert, 29; influence of, on incarnationalists, 83, 122–5
Bruno, Giordano, 15, 42, 45–6, 52, 102

Index

Bull, Bp. George, 108
Burke, Edmund, 55
Butler, Bishop, 63, 67, 73–4, 76, 127
Butts, Thomas, 34
Byron, Lord, 33, 89, 128

Cabbala, The, 9, 46–7
Calvinism, 58, 101
Cambridge, University of, alleged Platonism at, 8–9, 57, 73, 78–9, 82–4; alleged Scotism at, 121; Browning Society at, 122
Chadwick, Owen, 61
Charmides (Plato), 87
Chesterton, G. K., 126
Childhood, Romantics' interest in, 25–40, 68, 123
Christian Socialism, 113
Christian Social Union, 83, 122
Christmas Eve (Schleiermacher), 30
Christ's Hospital, 12, 14, 37, 47
Christus Veritas (Temple), 125
Church and State, Constitution of (Coleridge), 44, 99, 101, 105–6, 116–17
Church of England, Coleridge and Newman on, 58–9, 100
Cicero, on Aristotle's writings, 4
Clement of Alexandria, 70
Clerisy, Coleridge on, 71, 105, 115–18
Clough, A. H., 126
Coincidentia oppositorum, 41–56; as universal law, 6, 47–51; Coleridge's understanding of, 52–3, 100–10; in alchemical science, 47–8; in Protestant theology, 53–5; neoplatonic elaboration of, 45–7; origins of, 42; Platonic treatment of, 42–5; use of, by Romantics, 51–6
Colenso, Bishop, 127
Coleridge, Derwent, 38
Coleridge, Frank, 37
Coleridge, Hartley, 25–6; character of, 37–9; sonnet on birth of, 36
Coleridge, John, 32
Coleridge, Luke, 48
Coleridge, Samuel Taylor, 41, 77, 83, 86, 90, 111, 114, 122–4, 128; and *coincidentia oppositorum*, 42, 45, 48–9, 51–3, 55–6, 98–9, 127; and German thought, 12–13, 92–3, 97, 102–3; and Leibniz, 55; and Newman, 57–71; and Wordsworth's Immortality Ode, 25–7, 36–7; at Christ's Hospital, 12, 14, 47; epistemology of, 68, 92–4, 97–9; his concept of history, 60–61; his first knowledge of Blake, 36; his rejection of Locke, 14; his relations with Hartley, 37–9; his trichotomous logic, 52, 100–10; in-

fluence at Cambridge of, 78; on baptism and original sin, 30, 108; on children and education, 31–3, 68; on imagination, 15–16, 18, 20–24, 91–4; on Platonism and Aristotelianism, 1–3, 8–9, 13, 54; on Platonism and Plotinism, 7, 20; on Platonism in Christianity, 81–2; on Plato's method, 74; on the Clerisy, 105, 115–18; theology of, 81–2, 106–10, 112
Coleridge, Sara, 53
Collingwood, R. G., 61
Comte, Auguste, 81
Confessions of an Inquiring Spirit (Coleridge), 52, 106–7
Conjectura Cabbalistica (More), 47
Contemporary Review, The, 122
Contradictions, Coleridge on, 98–9; definition of, 95–6; in Plato, 43–4
Contraries, Blake's doctrine of, 44, 51, 97; Coleridge on, 44, 97–9, 103
Cory, William, 88
Critique of Pure Reason (Kant), 95–6
Cudworth, R., 22
Culler, Dwight, 63, 127
Culture and Anarchy (Arnold), 85, 127, 130

Dante, 65
Davy, Humphrey, 48
De Anima (Aristotle), 77
Dejection (Coleridge), 26
Delaura, David, 118, 126
Destiny of Nations (Coleridge), 36
Development, Newman's concept of, 62
Dialectic, 29, 43; Arnold's use of, 126; as intellectual progress, 56; as the mechanism of Coleridge's logic, 100–110; in modern theology, 53–4; Platonic definition of, 19–20, 61
Dionysius of Alexandria, 70, 122
Disciplina arcani, 71, 115
Discourses in America (Arnold), 127, 130
Döllinger, J. J. I. von, 61
Don Juan (Byron), 89
Dualism, 42, 46–7, 107

Economy, doctrine of, 70–71, 80, 130
Education, Arnold on, 130; Plato's theory of, 28–9; Romantics' distrust of, 31–4; Rousseau on, 30–31; Victorian axiom of, 117
Electrical Sciences, Coleridge on, 49, 99; origin and history of, 48–50
Élitism, of Arnold, 85, 130–31; of Coleridge, 115–18; of Newman, 118; of Plato, 6–7, 115–16; of the Romantics, 71

Index

Emerson, R. W., 9
Émile (Rousseau), 31
Emmett, Dorothy, 69
Empedocles on Etna (Arnold), 127
Empiricism, and induction, 74–5; of Aristotle and Locke, 2–3; Romantic revolt against, 13–15, 23
Encyclopaedia Metropolitana, 63
Endymion (Keats), 16, 18
Epistemology, and doctrine of antinomies, 95–9; and Romanticism, 2–3; of Aristotle, 4–7; of Coleridge, 68, 91–4; of M. Arnold, 126; of Newman, 66–70; of Plato, 4–7, 17, 19–20, 27–9; Romantic terminology of, 12–13
Erskine, Thomas, 112
Essay on Development (Newman), 62
Essays in Criticism (Arnold), 85
Essays of Elia (Lamb), 1
Eton College, 88
Euripides, 122
Euthydemus (Plato), 28, 43

Faith, Coleridge's definition of, 107; Maurice's definition of, 113; Scott Holland's definition of, 120
Faraday, Michael, 50
Farbenlehre (Goethe), 1
Fénélon, 36
Fenwick, Isabella, 26
Ficino, Marsilio, 27
Flaxman, John, 11
Fra Lippo Lippi (Browning), 123
France, Arnold's admiration for, 129
Fremantle, W. R., 121
Friend, The (Coleridge), 19–20, 37, 42, 49, 68, 91, 98, 101, 107, 115–16
Froude, R. H., 70
Frye, Northrop, 23
Fuseli, Henry, 11

Gautier, T., 86
Germany, 48, 68; and English Romanticism, 10–14; Coleridge in, 92; influence of, on Oxford thought, 77; Platonic revival in, 9–11; Platonic thought of, 18; Romantic concept of children in, 29–30
Gibbon, Edmund, 72
Gilbert, W. S., 1
Gilchrist, A., 20
Gladstone, Herbert, 74
Gladstone, W. E., 63, 76, 117; on Oxford 'Greats', 73–4
Goethe, J. W. von, 1, 9, 127; and alchemy, 10; on the child-philosopher, 29; wide-ranging studies of, 48–9

Gore, Charles, 83–4, 87–8, 119–22
Gorgias (Plato), 28; Hare's lectures on, 41
Grammar of Assent (Newman), 64–6
Grant, Sir Alexander, 119
Grasmere, 25
Gray, R. D., 10
'Greats' course at Oxford, *see* Oxford, University of
Greece, discovery of antiquities of, 11; early philosophy of, 42–3, 75, 119
Green, T. H., 77, 83, 87, 122; influence of, in Oxford, 119–21
Guérin, Maurice de, 128

Hare, Julius Charles, 8, 55–6, 78, 83; Platonism of, 41, 111
Harper, G. M., 13, 71
Harrow School, 83, 120, 122
Hegel, G. W., 9, 41, 55, 81, 83–4, 87, 102; dialectic of, 110; influence of, on Jowett, 77; on contradictions and antinomies, 96–7; on feeling and thought, 18; on magnetism and electricity, 49–50; on paradoxes, 52–3; on the child-philosopher, 29
Heine, Heinrich, 1
Hellas (Shelley), 9
Hellenism, in Romantic thought, 7, 9–11
Heraclitus, 42–3, 49, 79
Herculaneum, 11
Hermetic Tradition, and Romanticism, 9–10
Herrick, M. T., 127
Highgate, 78
Hipple, W. J., 126
Hirsch, E. D., 12
Hirst, Desirée, 10
History of the Arians (Newman), 70
Hogg, T. J., 35
Holland, Henry Scott, 83–4, 87–8, 119–22
'Holy Party' at Oxford, 83, 87–8, 119–125
Horace, 9
Hort, F. J. A., 83, 122
Hough, Graham, 59
Hutton, R. H., 111

Iamblichus, 12, 37, 103
Idea of a University (Newman), 64–5, 69, 78, 131
Idea of the Christian Church (Coleridge), 99
Idealism, philosophy of, 87–8
Illative sense, as defined by Newman, 67–8

165

Index

Illingworth, J. R., 120
Imagination, and neoplatonism, 70–71; as understood by Coleridge, 12, 15–24, 91–4; in children, 31–40; its relation to *anamnesis*, 25–6; Newman's concept of, 60; Romantics' use of, 15–18, 20–24
Immanentism, and incarnationalism, 80–81, 120
Immortality, Wordsworth's *Ode* on, 25–7, 36–7, 39. *See* also *anamnesis*
Incarnationalism, theology of, 79–83; and the 'Holy Party', 83–4, 87–8, 120–22; Browning as poet of, 83, 122–5; influence of T. H. Green on, 119–20
Induction, 61; in Aristotle and Plato, 74–5
Inge, W. R., 69, 81
Intuition, and children, 25–40, 123; as understood by Platonists, 5, 19–24, 92; in Newman and Coleridge, 68–9; Newman's distrust of, 59
Iremonger, F. A., 125

James, D. G., 128
Jena, Schelling's lectures at, 50
Jerusalem (Blake), 97
Johnson, E. D. H., 123
Johnson, Samuel, 60
Joubert, Joseph, 128, 130
Jowett, Benjamin, 17, 76–7, 84, 87
Justin Martyr, 79

Kant, Immanuel, 38, 77; antinomies of, 44, 95–7; Coleridge's opinion of, 3, 12–13, 102–3; Hegel on, 96–7; influence of, on Coleridge, 92–3
Kaufmann, Walter, 55, 96
Keats, John, 16–17
Keble, John, 70–71, 83
Kenosis, doctrine of, 83–4
Keswick, 48
King, Alec, 27
Kipling, Rudyard, 117
Klettenburg, S. von, 10
Knowledge, as a unity, 69; as power, 117. *See* also Epistemology
Kubla Khan (Coleridge), 14

Lamb, Charles, 1
Laplace, 49
Last Judgment, The (Blake), 22
Law, William, 10
Lay Sermons (Coleridge), 52, 101
Lay Sermons (Green), 120
Lectures on Justification (Newman), 59
Leibniz, G. W. von, 55
Leighton, Archbishop, 55

Lewis, Matthew Gregory, 14
Lightfoot, Bp. J. B., 122
Literary Remains (Coleridge), 104
Literature and Dogma (Arnold), 127
Locke, John, 2–3, 13, 15, 24, 47, 68; Coleridge's contempt for, 14, 57
Logic, and relation to antinomies, 95–6; Oxford training in, 63–4; Platonic and Aristotelian methods of, 74–5. *See* also Trichotomous Logic
Logic (Hegel), 18, 29, 50, 52–3
Logos, doctrine of, 79–82, 120–22
Loss and Gain (Newman), 64
Lowes, John Livingston, 14
Lucinde (Schlegel), 29
Ludlow, J. M., 113–14
Luther, Martin, 53
Lux Mundi (1889), 83, 88, 120, 122

Mackenzie, Henry, 11
Mad Monk, The (Coleridge), 25
Magnetism, and electricity, 49–50
Magus, Simon, 46
Manning, Cardinal H. E., 84
Marriage of Heaven and Hell (Blake), 51
Maurice, F. D., 33, 56, 64, 72, 77, 83, 89, 121, 123; and Westcott, 120, 122; his understanding of Platonism, 41–2, 54–5, 111–14; influence of, at Cambridge, 78–9; on Platonism and Aristotelianism, 1, 8–9, 57; on Platonism of children, 25, 28; on Plato's method, 74–5
McFaite, Ebenezer, 11
McFarland, Thomas, 92
Mean, Aristotle's doctrine of, 6, 52, 58–9, 100–01, 127
Mendelssohn, Moses, 11
Meno (Plato), 28
Mens Creatrix (Temple), 125
Merivale, Charles, 78
Methodus Theologia (Baxter), 102
Mill, John Stuart, 63, 77, 130; and élitism, 118; on Coleridge and Bentham, 56, 62; on Immortality Ode, 27; on Plato and Aristotle, 74–5
Milton (Blake), 97
Milton, John, 86
Moral and Metaphysical Philosophy (Maurice), 54
More, Aubrey, 120
More, Henry, 27, 47
Morley, John, 7, 31
Mozley, James, 67
Muir, Edwin, 39
Muirhead, J. H., 101
Mure, G. R. G., 84, 97

Index

Nature, Plato's and Aristotle's concept of, 5–6, 17; tendency to reunion within, 42, 46–7

Neoplatonism, 7–8, 23; and *anamnesis*, 27; and *coincidentia oppositorum*, 45–7, 97; and *disciplina arcani*, 70–71, 115; and *logos* doctrine, 79–80; Coleridge's knowledge of, 12, 103; contempt of Mill for, 75; influence of, on Newman, 70–71; in Thomas Taylor, 21; of Swedenborg and Blake, 11

Nettleship, R. L., 77

Newman, Francis, 86

Newman, John Henry, 8, 77–8, 83–4, 89, 123; and Coleridge, 57–72; his Aristotelianism, 58, 61–8, 69, 71–2; his concept of history, 60–61; his Platonism, 62, 68–71; M. Arnold's reverence for, 85–6, 126, 130–31; on élitism, 71, 118; on logic and rhetoric, 62–7; on the qualities of childhood, 30, 32–3, 39, 68

Newton, Isaac, 14, 34, 48, 127

Nicomachaean Ethics (Aristotle), 63, 73–78, 86, 100, 115, 119

Niebuhr, B. G., 67

Nightmare Abbey (Peacock), 15, 53

Northern Antiquities (Mallet), 14

Notebooks (Coleridge), 17–18, 24, 37, 98, 108

Notopoulos, J. A., 9

Novalis, F. von H., 9–10, 29

Occult, Romantics' interest in, 2, 9–11, 14, 46, 47

Oerstedt, 50

Ogilvie, R. M., 9

Optics, Romantics' study of, 48–9

Oriel College, Oxford, 63

Origen, 70, 81–3, 122, 125

Original Sin, Coleridge's views on, 30, 108

'Oxford Manner', origin of, 84, 87

Oxford Movement, 71, 80

Oxford, University of, alleged Thomism at, 121; Aristotelian training at, 8–9, 57, 63–5, 72–8, 127; contents of 'Greats' course at, 63–4, 73–4, 76–8, 84; cultural atmosphere of, 77–8, 84–8; growth of incarnationalism in, 83–4, 122; M. Arnold on, 84–6, 130–31; T. H. Green's teaching at, 119–20

Paget, Francis, 88

Paley, William, 66

Paracelsus, T. von H., 9, 15, 46–7

Paradox, as part of law of polarity, 43;

in Coleridge, 53, 108; in Hegel, 52–3; in M. Arnold, 126

Parmenides, 42–3, 45

Parmenides (Plato), 10, 17, 43–4, 95–6

Pater, Walter, 27

Pattison, Mark, 76

Peacock, Thomas Love, 11

Percival, Milton, 22, 46

Peterborough, 121–2

Phaedo (Plato), 11, 28, 35, 43, 87, 103

Phaedrus (Plato), 27, 73, 87, 130

Philebus (Plato), 19, 43, 52

Philo of Alexandria, 46, 79

Philosophical Lectures (Coleridge), 13–14, 69

Phronesis, and epistemology, 67–9; and Oxford education, 75–6; definition of, 5; in M. Arnold, 85

Pickwick, Mr Samuel, 2

Pietism, and Platonism, 9–10; in Schleiermacher, 30

Pippa Passes (Browning), 29, 123

Plato, and Aristotle, 4, 74–8, 87, 115; and élitism, 6–7, 115–16; and reconciliation theory, 42–6, 95–7; as studied at Oxford, 73–4, 76–7, 86–7; Blake on, 31; Byron on, 89; Coleridge on, 14, 37, 42, 45, 54; epistemology of, 4–7, 17, 19, 40, 68–71; Gladstone on, 74; his influence on Christian theology, 79–83; Holland's study of, 121; J. C. Hare on, 41; Jowett's study of, 77; M. Arnold on, 127–9; Maurice on, 41, 54; Westcott's respect for, 81–2, 122; Wordsworth's knowledge of, 26–7; W. Temple on, 125

Platonism, and *coincidentia oppositorum*, 42–6, 95–7; and historical method, 61; and incarnationalism, 79–83, 121–2; and Pietism, 9–10; and Romanticism, 9–15, 17, 19–21, 89–90; as applied to little children, 8–9, 25–40; at Cambridge, 8, 41, 57, 73; compared to Aristotelianism, 1–7, 13, 24; élitism of, 115–17; emergence of, at Oxford, 76–7, 83–8; in J. H. Newman, 62, 68–71; in T. H. Green, 119; Ludlow on, 113; of Browning, 123–4; of M. Arnold, 85–7, 126–31; of Maurice, 41–2, 111–14; revival of, in England, 11

Platonists, elaboration of Plato by, 4–7; in the seventeenth century, 3, 10–11, 45, 92, 108; of Alexandria, 70–71, 130; of the Renaissance, 6, 45

Plotinus, 10, 12, 16, 37; as elaborator of Plato, 7, 20

Poetics (Aristotle), 65, 73, 127

Index

Polarity, law of, *see Coincidentia oppositorum*
Politics (Aristotle), 73–4, 100, 115
Pompeii, 11
Poole, Thomas, 18, 32
Popper, Karl, 119
Pre-existence, *see Anamnesis*
Prelude (Wordsworth), 16, 26, 34, 36
Price, Bonamy, 39
Prichard, H. A., 77
Principles of Political Obligation (Green), 119
Proclus, 16, 27, 103
Prometheus Unbound (Shelley), 21
Protestant Theology, and *coincidentia oppositorum*, 53–5; Coleridge's sympathy with, 38
Pusey, E. B., 70, 83
Pythagoras, 42, 44, 52, 102–3

Raphael, 4
Reardon, B. M. G., 81
Reason, and Kant's teaching on antimonies, 95–7; and *Logos*, 79; and revelation, 59–60; and rhetoric, 66–8; as opposed to imagination, 91–4; as universal attribute, in Coleridge, 115; eighteenth-century concept of, 13–14
Reconciliation, Theories of, *see Coincidentia oppositorum*
Redemption, doctrine of, 80–81, 111
Reimarus, H. S., 33
Republic (Plato), 6, 9, 19, 21, 29, 36, 76–8, 79, 86, 115–16, 130–31
Rhetoric (Aristotle), 63, 73, 76
Richter, Melvin, 119
Robbins, William, 127
Robertson, F. W., 55
Robinson Crusoe (Defoe), 32
Robinson, H. Crabb, 11, 31, 36, 38; on Schelling, 50
Romanticism, and childish vision, 9, 25–40, 123; and *coincidentia oppositorum*, 6, 41–56, 96; and imagination, 15–24; and the occult, 2, 9–11, 14, 46–7; Arnold's criticism of poetry of, 127; epistemology of, 2–3, 14–18, 20–24; in Germany, 10–13, 29–30; in late nineteenth-century Oxford, 84–8; of Coleridge and Newman compared, 60–2, 68–71; Platonic origins of, 9–15
Rousseau, J. J., 30–31
Rudiments of Logic (Aldrich), 63
Ruskin, John, 17
Rydal Mount, 27

Saint John, admiration of Platonists

for, 121; Platonist influences on, 79–82; Westcott's study of, 82–3, 121–2;
W. Temple on, 125
Saint Paul, 46, 80–81
Schelling, F. W. J. von, 18, 24, 41, 42, 49; and Wordsworth, 12; Coleridge's debt to, 12–13, 92, 102; his lectures on electricity, 50
Schiller, J. C. F. von, 11
Schlegel, Friedrich, 10, 29
Schleiermacher, Friedrich, 10, 18, 24; on childish innocence, 30
Scholar-Gipsy, The (Arnold), 84
Schopenhauer, A., 9
Scott, Sir Walter, 60
Scotus, Erigena J., 42
Senancour, E. P. de, 128, 130
Sensationalism, Locke's philosophy of, 2, 14, 68
Sensibility, cult of, 30–31
Sermons in the Rolls Chapel (Butler), 63, 73–4
Sewell, William, 76
Shedd, W. E. T., 109
Shelley, P. B., 90, 123–4; and *anamnesis*, 35–6; Arnold on, 128; on imagination, 15–16; Platonism of, 9, 11, 17, 21
Simonides, paradoxes of, 43
Smith, Goldwin, 73
Smith, J. A., 77
Snyder, Miss A. D., 93, 106
Socinianism, 59
Socrates, 19, 27–9, 43, 52, 54, 84, 87–8, 103–4, 127
Socratic Method, definition of, 43–4, 74–5
Songs of Innocence and Experience (Blake), 34, 36
Sophist (Plato), 29, 43, 95
Sophocles, 86
Southey, Robert, 69, 99
Sparta, Plato on, 129
Spencer, Herbert, 81
Spenser, E., 21, 124
Spinoza, Benedict, 42, 126–7
Starkey, T., 47
Statesman (Plato), 17
Statue and the Beast, The (Browning), 124
Stedman, A. M. M., 77, 84
Stephenson, Joseph, 112
Strachey, Edward, 1, 8, 25, 72, 123
Street, T. G., 116
Swedenborg, Emmanuel, 11, 46–7, 51, 55, 110
'Sweetness and light', and élitism, 130–31; discussion of meaning of, 84–8; guardians of, 118
Sydenham, Floyer, 11, 35

Index

Symbolism, and Neoplatonism, 70–71; and sacraments, 60; in alchemy, 47; of Pythagoras, 103

Symposium (Plato), 11, 19, 45–6, 51, 80, 87, 130

Table Talk, Specimens of the (Coleridge), 1, 3, 13, 30–31, 48, 54–6, 61, 68, 81, 101, 105

Taoism, 51

Taylor, Thomas, x, 11, 21, 35, 70–71

Teleology, and Aristotle, 6, 62; F. W. Maurice's rejection of, 111; in M. Arnold, 127

Temple, William, 119, 124–5

Theaetetus (Plato), 43, 95

Thelwall, John, 31–2

Thirlwall, Connop, 78

Thomas Aquinas, 65

Tillich, Paul, 24

Timaeus (Plato), 10, 79

Tocqueville, Alexis de, 130

Tractarians, theology of, 71, 80

Trench, Abp. R. C., 78

Trichotomous logic, 52, 58, 100–10

Trilling, Lionel, 25, 126

Trinity College, Cambridge, 41

Trinity College, Oxford, 63

Trinity, doctrine of, and *Logos*, 79–80; Coleridge on, 52, 58, 106–10

Trusler, John, 34, 71

Tulk, C. A., 36, 42

Unitarianism, 58, 101, 106

United States of America, Arnold on, 129

Unity, importance of, in Browning, 124; Newman on, 62; of knowledge, 69; Romantics' preoccupation with, 16–18, 42, 48, 53; within trichotomous logic, 101–10

Urizon (Blake), 51

Valentine, Basil, 47

Vaughan, Henry, 27

Via media, as understood by Newman, 58–60

Volta, 49

Walsh, William, 16

Waterland, Daniel, 108

Wesley, Charles, 11

Wesley, John, 11

Westcott, B. F., 55; his admiration for Browning, 122–5; his relations with 'Holy Party', 83–4, 120–22; Platonism of, 79–83

Whately, Richard, 63, 65

Wilhelm Meister (Goethe), 29

Willey, Basil, 4

Wilson, Cook, 77

Winkelmann, J. J., 11

Wordsworth, Dorothy, 36, 38

Wordsworth, William, 29, 38, 60, 70, 86, 90, 123; and German thought, 12–13; and 'spots of time', 22; and T. H. Green, 119; his distrust of education, 31, 34; his first knowledge of Blake, 36; his Immortality Ode, 25–7, 36–7, 39; influence of, at Cambridge, 78; on imagination, 15–16; on Plato, 9, 26

Yates, Frances, 10

Young, G. M., 72, 78

Zeno, 42–3

Zuleika Dobson (Beerbohm), 87